THE
DISCIPLE'S WAY

Daily Reflections for Lent

THE
DISCIPLE'S WAY

Daily Reflections for Lent

Contributors:

Mark Francisco Bozzuti-Jones | Chris Corbin | Scott Gunn

Marcus George Halley | Deon K. Johnson | Everett Lees

Frank Logue | Troy Mendez | Hugo Olaiz | Anna Olson

Hillary Raining | Tyler Richards | Richard H. Schmidt

Stephen Smith | Jay Sidebotham | Kate E. Wesch | Joseph Yoo

FORWARD MOVEMENT
Cincinnati, Ohio

Cover and interior illustrations by Jason Sierra

Scripture quotations are from the New Revised Standard Version of the Bible, copyright ©1989 the National Council of the Churches of Christ in the United States of America.

Psalm quotations are from the Book of Common Prayer.

#2682

ISBN: 978-0-88028-525-4

© 2024 Forward Movement

Forward
Movement
inspire disciples. empower evangelists.

INTRODUCTION

Going Forward with High Adventure

Back in 1935, the very first publication of Forward Movement began by saying, "The Forward Movement is under way." On one level, this could have referred to the fact that a new organization was launching with an invigorating call for Lenten practice. But this opening line meant more.

In the mid-1930s, the Episcopal Church faced grave challenges. The church was anemic, lacking the money to fund its mission and the people to sustain its life. Unsure of how to respond, the General Convention of 1934 chartered the Forward Movement Commission to "reinvigorate the life of the church."

When the commission members gathered in late 1934 to decide how to accomplish their charge, they couldn't agree on how to proceed. In what was surely a Spirit-led insight, the first head of Forward Movement is reported to have said, "If we want the Episcopal Church to be strong, we need our congregations to be strong. And if we want our congregations to be strong, we need them to be filled not with habitual Christians, but with disciples of Jesus Christ."

So, the Forward Movement began with a bracing call to discipleship. In Lent of 1935, the first publication emerged. It was a bold summons to follow Jesus. In Lent 2025, we are celebrating 90 years of Forward Movement's ministry, but even more than that, we are giving thanks for nine decades of disciple-making, church renewal, and transformation of lives.

In this book, you will read the contents of the 1935 publication along with reflections from contemporary authors. We kept the King James Version of the daily scripture readings to accompany the meditations, but you can also find the New Revised Standard Version translation in the back of the book. We set the text from the original publication in highlighted boxes to make it easier to identify. The 1935 language is vigorous, and we asked our authors to adopt a similarly vigorous tone that might not be usual for today's church. But we need a stirring call to follow our Lord, a wake-up call.

DISCIPLESHIP

THE FORWARD MOVEMENT IS UNDER WAY

We Count on You to Join Us

FORWARD Movement means Discipleship for you. By Discipleship we step out and follow our Leader. This Manual seeks to put forward His claim. There is no substitute for Discipleship.

THIS GOING forward is high adventure. It isn't cheap and easy. If you enlist it will cost time, effort, pluck and money. If you care enough, you will pay the cost.

HOW TO START. Make up your mind. Start working with the rest of us on Ash Wednesday, March 6th. Follow this Manual step by step. Give a piece of every day to it—if only 10 minutes. Give more as you are led to deeper thinking and reading. Hold on gamely.

"There is no substitute for discipleship. This going forward is high adventure. It isn't cheap and easy. If you enlist, it will cost time, effort, pluck, and money. If you care enough, you will pay the cost." That's what they said in 1935, and it's still true today.

The Lent booklet of 1935 featured a woodcut of a ship with seven sails. The seven sails doubtless recalled the seven steps of discipleship: turn, follow, learn, pray, serve, worship, share. The imagery of a ship is commonly used for the church: the church is a refuge, a safe place in stormy waters. But in this case, the woodcut helps us picture the church not as a static place but as a community of disciples on the move.

In traditional church architecture, the place where the people sit is called the nave. This word comes from the same origins as "naval," and it takes its name in part because the pointed roof can be seen as an upside-down ship. When we come to church, we are gathering in a kind of ship. Ships fulfill their purpose when they travel, sometimes on stormy seas. And the church fulfills its purpose when it moves forward, sometimes amidst great challenges.

Perhaps the greatest spiritual danger in this day and age is complacency. It's tempting to delude ourselves into thinking that we can fit our Christian faith into the gaps of a comfortable consumer lifestyle. It's easy to lose the plot and think that church is primarily a place for comfort, not a place of transformation.

We need a vigorous push, both as individuals and as a church. Jesus rightly said that we cannot serve two masters. Either we choose to follow him, or we do not. My prayer and fervent hope are that we will put Jesus first. I hope you will find this Lenten devotional book helpful in rekindling—or beginning—your journey as a disciple of Jesus Christ.

You will encounter a variety of voices among the authors here, all ably edited by Richelle Thompson. Jason Sierra has created new cover art to recall the 1935 art and to inspire us afresh. Above all else, I pray that our church will be stirred to carry out the work that our Lord has given us to do, to make disciples of all nations. It will not be easy, but that is the adventure of discipleship. And we are never alone, for Jesus has promised to be with us until the end of the age.

Have a holy and stirring Lent.

Scott Gunn
Cincinnati, Ohio
Feast of St. Philip and St. James 2024

THE FORWARD MOVEMENT IS UNDER WAY

We Count on You to Join Us

Forward Movement means discipleship for you. By discipleship, we step out and follow our leader. This manual seeks to put forward this claim. There is no substitute for discipleship. This going forward is high adventure. It isn't cheap and easy. If you enlist, it will cost time, effort, pluck, and money. If you care enough, you will pay the cost.

HOW TO START. Make up your mind. Start working with the rest of us on Ash Wednesday. Follow this manual step by step. Give a piece of every day to it—if only 10 minutes. Give more as you are led to deeper thinking and reading. Hold on gamely.

FIRST FOUR DAYS IN LENT
A DISCIPLE TURNS

What they did, we can do. They lived in times worse than ours, more cruel, more hopeless. These first disciples were men and women like us—everyday humanity. Jesus comes near and beckons to them. They turn to him, give him their attention. Just that at first. Yet what they do—stop, turn, take him in—puts us forever in their debt. They started discipleship. Look at our world: a mad scramble for security, where the strong trample the weak. Look at yourself. "Each man feels the thing he might be, beating beneath the thing that he is." You are not content. How to become what you might be? That's the question. I can't lift myself by my own bootstraps. I must have help.

Through the world's racket and the pulse of one's own dissatisfaction, Christ keeps saying: "I am the way. Turn to Me. I am here to help you."

Stop in your tracks. Turn around. Look! Christ is there. What do you care that he doesn't register on eyes and ears? Only the very first ever got him that way. He is in your heart. His face and voice are in the Gospels. Get hold of the little book. Wring his meaning out of it. Ask someone. The church proclaims him. Stop. Turn around. Consider Him.

PRAY: Christ, help me to turn from self and find you.
AFFIRM: I will face Christ and give him a fair chance.
DO THIS: Trust your impulse to stop and turn. This week, read Saint Mark's Gospel. Wring the meaning out of it—the good news it has for you.

 TURNS

The Week of Ash Wednesday

Ash Wednesday

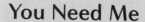

You Need Me

Behold, I stand at the door, and knock; if any man hear my voice, and open the door, I will come in to him, and will sup with him, and he with me.

—REVELATION 3:20

It came to pass, as Jesus sat at meat in the house, behold many publicans and sinners came and sat down with him and his disciples. And when the Pharisees saw it, they said unto his disciples, Why eateth your Master with publicans and sinners? But when Jesus heard that, he said unto them, They that be whole need not a physician, but they that are sick.... I am not come to call the righteous, but sinners to repentance.

—MATTHEW 9:10-12, 13B

When Jesus said, "I have come to call not the righteous but sinners," he was making it clear: "I have come to call all y'all." The call was for everyone, as no one is fully righteous on their own. Jesus began his public ministry with a brief proclamation to all who would listen about making this discipleship turn:

"The time is fulfilled, and the kingdom of God has come near; repent, and believe in the good news."

To repent is to look back on wrong past actions, feel remorse, confess to God, and then change our behavior going forward. On Ash Wednesday, we are offered space to recall the ways in which we see we have messed up, fallen short, or hurt others out of our own wounds. The Book of Common Prayer gives us these words in the prayer for the day, "Create and make in us new and contrite hearts, that we, worthily lamenting our sins and acknowledging our wretchedness, may obtain of you, the God of all mercy, perfect remission and forgiveness."

This is not about beating ourselves up, as the heart of this love message is offering us a "do over," a second chance, or third or fourth or hundredth. The most common word for sin in scripture means "to miss the mark." This was a term used in archery for not hitting the bullseye. The goal we are to be aiming for is God's will for our lives. Scripture makes it clear that we can miss, not because our aim is slightly off but because we are using a different target. In this season of Lent, we see that there is more to the discipleship turn than looking back with regret. We also get to take fresh aim.

This is where a word about translation can deepen our understanding. The word for repent in the Greek text of Mark's Gospel is *metanoia*, which means to have an "after mind"—a mind reconfigured after a metamorphosis. We usually refer to this type of transformation as a change of heart and mind. Translators like to opt for the most economical way of conveying a concept with a single word standing in for another single word. So, they used the word repent to convey the meaning of a change in how someone sees the world and their place in it.

This conversion is what happened when an encounter with Jesus caused someone to know him for who he is and to fall in love. The first followers had already seen how the maker of heaven and earth is present in Jesus, the Messiah. But when they learn Jesus cares about them and wants them to be with him, that changes everything. Their lives will never be the same after his invitation to go deeper in their faith.

Andrew, Simon Peter, James, and John will leave their fishing nets, not out of regret for their past sins but out of hope for what life with Jesus could be. The change captured by the word *metanoia* is nothing less than regeneration, a new birth that leads to new thoughts and actions, not driven by fear but responding to love. This moment of recognition of the truth of the Good News of Jesus would change the heart of Mary Magdalene, who became the apostle to the apostles after Jesus's resurrection. Down through the centuries, we see saints in every age in whose lives we find a *metanoia*, a revolution, that took over their hearts and minds, after which life was never, ever the same. With converted minds, they set their mark as God's will.

The life-changing, heart-transforming Good News at the heart of Christianity is that you matter to the maker of the cosmos. Once you see that there is a creator God who does not stand back like a mildly curious clockmaker or a stern judge but a loving God who cares for you as the best of loving parents care for their child, then everything is different. We can find healing and wholeness in Jesus and let past pains go as we look forward in faith to a life lived with the awareness that God is with us and will never forsake us. In a world of wounded people going on to hurt others, this is the best news ever.

—*Frank Logue*

Thursday

How Much Do You Care?

Behold, a sower went forth to sow; And when he sowed, some seeds fell by the wayside, and the fowls came and devoured them up: Some fell upon stony places, where they had not much earth: and forthwith they sprung up, because they had no deepness of earth: And when the sun was up, they were scorched; and because they had no root, they withered away. And some fell among thorns; and the thorns sprung up and choked them: But others fell into good ground, and brought forth fruit ... Who hath ears to hear, let him hear.

—Matthew 13:3b-9

A good gardener knows the importance of turning over soil. They will take the time to till the land to refresh nutrients, oxygen, and minerals in preparation for the ground to receive new seeds. In our passage today, the sower distributes seeds that produce fruits of many spiritual kinds. Clearly, he plans to spread this seed no matter what type of soil he encounters, with the hope that our hearts will be fertile ground for the seeds to flourish and thrive.

As disciples, we turn the soil of our hearts by engaging in spiritual practices such as participation in the sacraments, scripture reading, and prayer. But there is a subtle warning here that we disciples should heed. The more of these practices we do, the richer and more fertile the soil of our hearts becomes. This growth is wonderful if we let God plant the seeds of love, peace, and justice that the Holy Spirit desires for this world. But if we plant other seeds of power, prestige, personal security, etc., they will likewise grow and flourish. No matter what seeds are planted, they will grow in well-tilled soil. Ironically, soil that is not tilled at all may be in less danger of producing negative fruits because it is not likely to produce much fruit. Thus, we need to be sure to return to the sower over and over again.

One way to return to God is through the pastoral rite called Reconciliation of a Penitent (also known as private confession). This service is an excellent tool in our work of returning. In fact, the whole idea of reconciliation is that we come to the cross to lay down the sins we have been carrying, to lay them at the foot of the cross, and then to turn around and return to the life God has called us to. In private confession, we are given the gift of pruning away the fruits that are the byproducts of the self-serving seeds we have planted in our lives. In confession, we are given a safe place to release the things weighing us down by confessing the places in our lives where we need help, guidance, and then reassurance of our beloved status as children of God. As we begin this first week of Lent, let this be an invitation to consider calling your priest and engaging in this freedom-giving practice and turn again to God so that our hearts may be ready to accept the seeds of the Spirit.

—*Hillary Raining*

Friday

Simple? Troubled? Welcome.

At that time Jesus answered and said, I thank thee, O Father, Lord of heaven and earth, because thou hast hid these things from the wise and prudent, and hast revealed them unto babes. Even so, Father: for so it seemed good in thy sight. All things are delivered unto me of my Father: and no man knoweth the Son, but the Father; neither knoweth any man the Father, save the Son, and he to whomsoever the Son will reveal him. Come unto me, all ye that labour and are heavy laden, and I will give you rest. Take my yoke upon you, and learn of me; for I am meek and lowly in heart; and ye shall find rest unto your souls. For my yoke is easy and My burden is light.

—MATTHEW 11:25-30

Growing up in Texas in the 1980s, I realized at a young age that being part of a church was simply a facet of society. If you lived in an area that was predominantly Christian, it was often assumed by your neighbors that you were also a Christian. In that way, people lived in very similar ways to one another, and cultural norms were clearly established, sometimes quite prominently and other times in unwritten ways. This type of "Christian" society kept people thinking, acting, and doing things in similar ways. It wasn't until I was in college that I recognized that American culture has a great deal more variety of religious thought, practices, and lifestyles.

The first-century religious establishment in Jerusalem held a firm belief that the only way to know God and to love God was to follow a strict set of ordinances and practices that must be obeyed at all times. Adherence to these precepts was of utmost importance. Some of these practices were so rigid that they kept people from having any kind of spiritual experience of God at all. Jesus's ministry sought to clarify how these practices were originally intended to serve God and God's way of love, but he also was very quick to show how aspects of these religious norms detracted people from recognizing the presence of the Living God in their lives. Even though the leaders of the religious establishment expected all people to adhere to their interpretation of God's law, many who were poor, sick, illiterate, or disabled were not always able to comply. Jesus identified the lack of compassion in the law and sought to teach his disciples another way to live a life of love, loving God fully and loving our neighbors as ourselves. Instead of focusing on following the law, Jesus invited his disciples to follow him.

When I began recognizing the diversity of religious beliefs and practices in society, I realized that I had always approached my faith in a very passive way. Sure, I went to church and said my prayers, but learning to follow Jesus and his way of love was a completely different dimension of life. The life of a disciple requires a person to turn toward the love God has for us.

We turn toward God's love when we follow Jesus, but this takes a great deal of concentration and effort. When I made the deliberate decision to follow a path of discipleship, I began reading more about Jesus. I started spending long periods of time reflecting on God's purposes for me. I knew I needed a deeper understanding of the Bible and how it has informed the Church since the beginning. After all, when anyone changes certain aspects of their life and how they see the world, a whole new framework of habits and practices must be established to orient oneself to a new way of life. There's a *metanoia* involved: a need to turn toward a new way to be.

The most important and most valuable aspect of knowing and following Jesus is recognizing that we are always with him, and he is always with us. When things get difficult, Jesus can lead us by his yoke. He can give us rest for our souls, even in moments of significant challenge. His gentleness and meekness make us receptive and teachable. Jesus extends an open invitation for us to follow. When we do, we see how we are always together with him, and he is always with us.

—*Troy Mendez*

Saturday

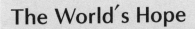

The World's Hope

And he turned him unto his disciples, and said privately, Blessed are the eyes which see the things that ye see; For I tell you, that many prophets and kings have desired to see those things which ye see, and have not seen them; and to hear those things which ye hear, and have not heard them.

—LUKE 10:23-24

Jesus answered and said unto her, Whosoever drinketh of this water shall thirst again: But whosoever drinketh of the water that I shall give him shall never thirst; but the water that I shall give him shall be in him a well of water springing up into everlasting life.

—JOHN 4:13-14

To be a Christian is to be a person who offers hope: a hope based on the life, death, and resurrection of Jesus Christ. Hope in Jesus Christ orders the human imagination and mode of living in the world. At the same time, we seek and desire a world built on justice and modeled on the teachings of Jesus Christ.

Hope in the Christian experience lives on by acknowledging how blessed we are to have spiritual ancestors who encountered Jesus, how blessed we are to live in the life of Christ now, and how blessed we are to know that God will be with us in our future. Jesus Christ says to us what he said to his disciples: "Blessed are the eyes which see the things that ye see." In Jesus, we see God's saving words and acts that bring life and love into the world.

Christian hope allows us to drink from the water, "a well of water springing up into everlasting life." To be a Christian is to be a person of hope; it is a hope that invites us to be the light of the world. Christian hope springs up in us like a well of water; because of it, we commit to a life that brings peace and justice to all. The hope we have in Jesus Christ always points us to eternal life. Eternal life shows itself in our present reality through how we feed the hungry, visit the sick, give drink to the thirsty, and pay loving attention to the poor.

What does it mean for us to be a people of hope? Expectation. Trust. Desire. At the center of the spiritual life, alongside faith and love, is the virtue of hope. Both a verb and noun, hope calls us to expect the presence of God in ourselves, our neighbors, and every human being. To expect to be the hope, love, and presence of God in myself and every human being is a game changer in the spiritual life, moving us from expecting to trusting. Faith and hope are the wings of love. In truth, hope would never exist without love.

Jesus reveals to the disciples how blessed they are to have the hopes of all the world in their very presence. Jesus Christ is the desire of every human hope because we believe he is the creator of all that is—seen and unseen. Part of hope is knowing that we will meet Jesus face-to-face one day. This is our deepest and strongest hope.

Christians are at their most authentic self when they point to Jesus Christ as the world's best hope. In Jesus, we find and learn the way to be good news to the poor and oppressed. Hope in Jesus Christ motivates us to love and work on behalf of the most vulnerable in our midst. The true disciple of Christ undermines the lies of our society that tell us that some lives have greater value than others. When our hope is founded on God, we build our lives on the truth that God is love. Hope reminds us of this truth: we cannot love God, whom we cannot see, if we do not love those we see. May our hope in Jesus Christ lead us to do what is good, true, and beautiful. Christian hope points to the power and life-changing and saving impact on Jesus, who loves this world.

—*Mark Francisco Bozzuti-Jones*

FOLLOWS

First Week in Lent

A DISCIPLE FOLLOWS

Christ is going forward. Are you with him before distance parts you? Decide to follow! Step out after him. He lives your life if you try to live his. Now that you get going with your eyes on him, your old job, the old duty is a new thing. His purpose instead of the old drifting. No longer "What pleases me?" or "What pleases people?" but "What says Christ?" You are Christ's partner.

Remember, it is only one step at a time. He never abandons even the most stumbling disciple. He begins to control the look on my face, the thoughts in my head, the things I choose and do. As his partner, I find I must redivide my time, my interests, my strength, my money; none for this, less for that, much more for something else. Master, you've started something in me. It hurts often but keep me with you. My partner has no use for my fearfulness, my old trick of dodging the issue, shading off the truth. It is hard to let all these shabby, hidden things go. It's a showdown. My old self or new in Christ.

PRAY: Help me to follow you this day.

AFFIRM: I have enlisted as Christ's disciple.

DO THIS: Before you say or do something, ask yourself, "Is Christ my partner, with me in this? Does he indicate a different way?" With your regular work done, look for the extra thing he wants you to do.

You are a disciple of Jesus, and that means following Jesus in all ways. In our modern world, this can feel countercultural, antiquated, or simply uncool. The assignment for Christians is radical, transformational, and life-changing! We must keep our minds focused on Christ and doing his will, even and perhaps especially when it means doing things differently from those around us. As disciples of Jesus, we must set aside fear, anxieties, and self-conscious worries to see the truths and face them.

I am a parent to two adolescents, and recently, something very unsettling happened with my younger son. He plays hockey on a competitive travel team. He's 10 years old, and already, his devotion to this sport requires approximately twenty hours per week for seven months out of the year. It's intense.

In the last week of the season, the kids play a final tournament, and emotions run high for coaches, players, and parents alike. All the hard work of the past months comes to a head, and it feels like so much is riding on these final games.

After a tough loss in a tournament game, I watched as these 9- and 10-year-old children turned against one another. In the locker room following the game, they began blaming one another for the loss. Their words were unkind, negative, and hurtful. Some children were upset; others joined in the teasing, while most remained silent. And, in the midst of it all, I witnessed an adult yelling at a child to "shut up." I can't make this up.

We can roll our eyes at the intensity of youth sports, modern parenting techniques, or any number of social ills that contributed to this sad scene, but I see it as a sobering example.

These children are echoing what they see. At this age, their behavior mimics their parents, grandparents, teachers, and coaches. This locker room scene is a microcosm of our society at large.

When things go wrong, we turn against one another. I'm not talking about major trauma but rather the everyday incidences of setbacks and disappointment. When this happens, some people become mean, violent, and aggressive. Some people are tender, hurt, and scared. Others remain silent but not unaffected.

As we debriefed this awful experience, I told my son that we never know what has happened to people or what is going on in their lives. The kid who is a bully is probably being bullied. The mean neighbor or grumpy co-worker might be sick, in pain, or grieving.

It doesn't make it okay to treat others poorly, but we can have patience and compassion.

We must work every day to embody what it means to be a disciple. It may seem obvious that we don't want to be the ones using our voices and bodies to lash out in anger or violence. But what do we do when we witness that behavior? When this happens, we have a choice. We get to choose how we wish to respond in our words, actions, and facial expressions. Do we intervene? Do we remain passive?

We wish to follow Jesus, and Jesus does not abandon us. If Jesus does not abandon us, how do we ensure we will not abandon him? What can we do to ensure we are the parent, grandparent, coach, or teacher standing up for justice and righteousness?

It begins with daily prayer and the study of scripture. Going to church on Sundays is simply not enough. We must intentionally and regularly build our spiritual muscles by developing our minds and hearts and nurturing our souls.

—*Kate E. Wesch*

Monday of the First Week in Lent

Here is Certainty

Now when John had heard in the prison the works of Christ, he sent two of his disciples, And said unto him, Art thou he that should come, or do we look for another? Jesus answered and said unto them, Go and shew John again those things which ye do hear and see: The blind receive their sight, and the lame walk, the lepers are cleansed, and the deaf hear, the dead are raised up, and the poor have the gospel preached to them. And blessed is he, whosoever shall not be offended in me.

MATTHEW 11:2-6

I spend most of my time and vocation among the demographic the church desperately wants (and needs) to understand: young adults. Young adults have come of age at a time when most of the systems and institutions that previous generations took for granted have all but crumbled. Everything from family, homeownership, and economic opportunities to religious and political institutions to the planet's future feels like it is built on sand that is quickly eroding. From this standpoint, certainty—particularly as it relates to something as mysterious as faith—feels almost laughable at best and insulting at worst.

As I write this reflection, I am walking with a student preparing for baptism. She grew up in a nominally Roman Catholic household, but unlike her siblings, she was never baptized, and her family never attended church services. She began attending chapel services because she joined the chapel choir. Her conversion story resembles the slow burn of a new fire. It started small—feeling connected to certain parts of the liturgy or particular pieces of music—and eventually came to incorporate big questions. When I asked what faith meant to her, she said, "I can't make sense of everything I read in the Bible or we say in chapel, but something about that calls to me. I believe it *enough* to give it my life and let it guide me." I found the phrase "I believe it enough" deeply resonant, and it has helped me better wrap my mind around the faith Jesus asks of those who follow him.

John the Baptizer asks Jesus, "Are you the one, or should we wait for another?" It is an important question. John is in prison. Given his relationship with Herod, he likely knows his days are numbered. His question is motivated by his concern about his fledgling religious movement and—perhaps more importantly—the kingdom of God to which his movement points. I hear in John's question someone primed to give themselves away if only they could have some assurance that Jesus is the one for whom they have been waiting.

John the Baptizer, revered in Christian history, sounds much like many of us. Jesus responds to John by highlighting the mountain of evidence that God is on the move, in language that seems to allude to the prophet Isaiah's depiction of the year of Jubilee: the afflicted are healed, the dead are raised to life, and the poor have good news brought to them. The message here is: if you're looking for God, look for the signs that God has been here.

In a world of so much uncertainty, where it can be challenging to know what to believe, those who follow Jesus must learn to discern the signs of his presence. How do we know that Jesus is here? We will know he is here because we see love among people, particularly among supposed enemies. When Jesus is present, we will see joy bubbling up in unexpected places. Where Jesus is, there is peace built on vulnerability, not violence. The signs of his presence include kindness, goodness, faithfulness, gentleness, and self-control. If you haven't picked up what I am putting down, these are the fruits of the Spirit. Our work is to discern the signs of his presence in the world around us and cultivate them within ourselves. We are the sacrament of Christ's ongoing presence in the world. The kingdom of God begins with us. We are salt. We are light. We are a city built on a hill. We are messengers of the gospel, witnesses of the Resurrection, whose work is to bring this resurrection reality into the lives of everyone around us.

—*Marcus George Halley*

Tuesday of the First Week in Lent

Meant For Us All

And in the morning, rising up a great while before day, he went out, and departed into a solitary place, and there prayed. And Simon and they that were with him followed after him. And when they had found Him, they said unto Him, All men seek for thee. And he said unto them, Let us go into the next towns, that I may preach there also: for therefore came I forth.

MARK 1:35-38

In the 25 verses preceding today's reading from Mark's Gospel, Jesus traveled, presumably on foot, to four (possibly five) different places, was baptized, tempted in the wilderness, called four disciples, taught in the synagogue, cast out an unclean spirit, healed Peter's mother-in-law of a fever, and then healed lots more people and cast out many more demons. The word immediately occurs eight times in these 25 verses. All that rushing about surely exhausted Jesus. It exhausts me just to read about it. No wonder Jesus got up in the middle of the night and went off to find a place where he could be alone.

For much of my life, I felt that way, too. The duties of job, family, and community seemed to grow heavier every year. I tried to follow Jesus, and I managed to block out a bit of time most days for Bible reading and prayer, but those efforts were often rushed, and my to-do list for the day pushed God to the sidelines of my mind. I hoped to get by on good intentions. "Be still, and know that I am God," the psalmist advises. Really? How was I to do that?

It's different nowadays. I am retired. In some ways, following Jesus seems easier now. I sit quietly for 30 to 40 minutes each morning to pray and reflect on the scriptures and devotional literature, and my mind doesn't wander as often. I don't know that I'm following Jesus more faithfully now than in my younger years, but I enjoy a sense of serenity and contentment that I hadn't known before. I finally found that "solitary place" I only dreamt of before. I hope Jesus found the same when he got up in the middle of the night and went off to be alone.

What did Jesus do when he found his solitary place? It says he prayed. How did Jesus pray? He taught his disciples to pray, and we recite what he taught them at every worship service. But Jesus surely did more than rattle off the Lord's Prayer. He didn't have a prayer book or a rosary. Maybe he called to mind all the people he had taught, healed, and delivered from demons. Maybe he just breathed deeply, looked at the stars, said "Thank you," and dozed off. All of that can be seen as prayer, and any of it would be a good use of time in a solitary place.

But then Jesus's quiet time was interrupted. The disciples found him. "Everybody's looking for you!" they said. "Well, yes, I suppose so," Jesus said (if I may paraphrase him). "So, let's go to the next towns so that I can preach there, too. That's what I came here for." And Jesus went back to preaching and casting out demons. As for me, I now try to follow Jesus "on to the next towns" through the volunteer work I do with the sick, the lonely, and the destitute.

Following Jesus means seeking a rhythm or balance between actively serving God and being refreshed in our solitary place. Jesus presumably found that rhythm and balance. Sometimes, it's easier to find it than at other times, which seems to have been true for Jesus as well. When you manage to find this balance, enjoy it and give thanks for it. When you can't, know that you are loved just the same, take one moment at a time, trust the grace of God to enable you to carry on, and maintain a sense of humor about it all. Wait patiently, and there will come a time when you will find your solitary place.

—*Richard H. Schmidt*

Wednesday of the First Week in Lent

Quibbles Can't Stop Him

And he entered again into the synagogue; and there was a man there which had a withered hand. And they watched him, whether he would heal him on the sabbath day; that they might accuse him. And he saith unto the man which had the withered hand, Stand forth. And he saith unto them, Is it lawful to do good on the sabbath days, or to do evil? to save life or to kill? But they held their peace. And when he had looked round about on them with anger, being grieved for the hardness of their hearts, he saith unto the man, Stretch forth thine hand. And he stretched it out; and his hand was restored whole as the other.

MARK 3:1-5

Years ago, fresh out of college, I worked as a union organizer. At one point, we were supporting workers in a factory that made cute baby products, things like bottles and pacifiers with characters printed on them. The workers made minimum wage year after year without even a single paid sick day. Supervisors yelled and cursed them while they worked. And the company had just become caught in a scandal, where recalled products that were dangerous to babies were simply repackaged for sale without fixing the problem. The workers decided to take their case to the consumer. We went from mall to mall, seeking out stores that sold the products. Then, right in the middle of the shopping mall, we'd start to chant. Loudly. While a few of us got people's attention, others passed out information and engaged people in conversation, asking them to take action to protest working conditions and safety violations.

The first time I yelled at the top of my lungs in the middle of a public indoor space, I couldn't believe I was doing it. It turned out nothing was stopping me, although a tired-looking security guard eventually wandered over and suggested that I pipe down. I realized something strange—that the only reason we weren't all making crazy noise in shopping malls and other public spaces was because we just knew we weren't supposed to. And at heart, many of us don't like breaking the rules or standing out in a crowd. Or, we don't even think about the rules because they seem so obvious and absolute.

Any follower of Jesus in Galilee lived and breathed the Sabbath and its restrictions nearly as naturally as the air. The whole community observed the Sabbath and their very ways of being and doing had been adapted to make this possible. The idea of challenging the Sabbath likely never occurred to those early disciples. What to us may look like an obvious choice—heal the person, rules aside!—wasn't obvious at all. I'm not even sure there was a clear need to violate the laws of Sabbath in this instance. While I don't know exactly what a withered hand entailed, it doesn't sound like an emergency condition. No one is bleeding to death or struggling to breathe. No heart has stopped. This hand, one imagines, had been this way before the encounter with Jesus and would continue in more or less the same condition after the Sabbath sun went down. I can't blame the onlookers for their reaction; I might well have been among them.

The introduction for this week mentions that Jesus is on the move, sometimes leaving us struggling to keep up. Let's try to imagine our way into this story as modern disciples. What are some things that we just absolutely, one hundred percent assume are the right ways of doing things? What would we do, say, or feel if Jesus upended one of those things? Most of us don't observe orthodox Sabbath restrictions, but we assume all kinds of things about how church is supposed to be, how people are supposed to act in specific contexts, and what things should not be broken or rearranged. If Jesus just started doing something totally unexpected, would we be able to keep up? Would we need to understand why he was doing it, or could we trust that it was part of a larger plan? Might Jesus mess with some of our most closely held beliefs and traditions just to get us to pay attention to something more important?

The next time someone proposes a change that seems wrong, the next time you see someone acting strange or foolish, try imagining that the disruption might be calling your attention to something more important, something that matters to Jesus and needs to matter to us.

—*Anna Olson*

Thursday of the First Week in Lent

Right At Any Cost

And they come to Jerusalem: and Jesus went into the temple, and began to cast out them that sold and bought in the temple, and overthrew the tables of the moneychangers, and the seats of them that sold doves; And would not suffer that any man should carry any vessel through the temple. And he taught, saying unto them, Is it not written, My house shall be called of all nations the house of prayer? but ye have made it a den of thieves. And the scribes and chief priests heard it, and sought how they might destroy him.

MARK 11:15-18A

The story of Jesus clearing the temple appears in each of the gospels, which tells us that it's a story to which we need to pay attention. In John's Gospel, the story appears at the beginning of Jesus's ministry, providing a lens through which to examine the entire gospel. In the other three gospels, the story appears right before Holy Week, where it becomes, as Mark tells us, one of the reasons that authorities needed to get rid of Jesus.

And what was his offense? It was seeking to preserve the sanctity of the temple as a house of prayer, for all the nations.

Moneychangers and others had turned it into a marketplace, missing the point of the temple. This story represents Jesus's encounter with the intertwined systems of his day—religious, political, and economic. It shows his willingness to act boldly and decisively against those systems defended by scribes and chief priests, the religious elite.

As we focus this week on the disciple's call to follow Jesus, this story challenges us to think about the systems at work in our world, especially those that present obstacles to nurturing justice and peace. We see those systems at work in our politics, race relations, discrimination against persons because of sexual orientation, and the plight of immigrants. We find ourselves recalling the history of our nation marked by slavery, racial divide, and genocide of Indigenous people. Tragically, we can't deny that what Martin Luther King Jr. noted about church is still true. In our society, Sunday morning is still the most segregated hour of our week. These experiences call us, as Jesus's followers, to take a stand, as we remember that Jesus came to comfort the afflicted and afflict the comfortable.

The story also comes as a challenge to consider how we participate in those systems. If Jesus showed up in our community, maybe our church, would he start turning over tables? If Saint Paul was still in the letter-writing business, what would he say about our religious institutions today? About your church and mine? As we consider this week's theme about following Jesus, as that builds on last week's theme of turning (or repentance), there may be ways that we need to repent this Lent from our complicity in systems that are unjust, systems that draw us from the love of God and stand in the way of God's gracious kingdom extended to all persons. Our silence about these systematic injustices can constitute complicity.

And there is another way to think about how this story of cleansing the temple applies to us as individuals in our journey of faith as disciples. We can read this story mindful that, as Saint Paul says, we each are a temple of the Holy Spirit. If that is the case, what tables does Jesus need to overturn in our inner life? What are the movements of our hearts that keep us from following Jesus? Have we lost focus on what the temple is all about? This week, we focus on discipleship as expressed in our call to follow Jesus. We are invited to consider the ways that the temple of our hearts might be cleared, how the institutions that shape our common life may need to be challenged and reformed, and at the same time, how our inner lives can become houses of prayer.

This disruptive activity by Jesus, either as described in the gospels or realized in our own day, is not simply a matter of Jesus's angry judgment. It is intended to clear the way and remove obstacles that keep us from more faithful discipleship. It is meant to invite us into a deeper, loving relationship with God. So, we ask Jesus to come again and cleanse the temple, clear the house of God, and maybe, in the process, turn over a few tables so that we might see him more clearly, love him more dearly, and follow him more nearly,
day by day.

—*Jay Sidebotham*

Friday of the First Week in Lent

Servant of All

He riseth from supper, and laid aside his garments; and took a towel, and girded himself. After that he poureth water into a bason, and began to wash the disciples' feet, and to wipe them with the towel wherewith he was girded . . . So after he had washed their feet, and had taken his garments, and was set down again, he said unto them, Know ye what I have done to you? Ye call me Master and Lord: and ye say well; for so I am. If I then, your Lord and Master, have washed your feet; ye also ought to wash one another's feet. For I have given you an example, that ye should do as I have done to you.

JOHN 13:4-5, 12-15

Feet are a part of the body we rarely think about—except when they are smelly or hurt! I have been thinking a lot about my own feet since January when I came down with painful, debilitating plantar fasciitis. I have experienced this ailment before, but never have I hurt so much or spent so much time just unable to walk. Despite my best efforts, which included attending sessions of physical therapy, buying several exercise gadgets, and taking daily doses of painkillers, the pain has continued, uninterrupted, for three months.

When we lived in Chapel Hill, North Carolina, my husband and I attended Maundy Thursday services in a large cabin in a nearby forest. This cabin was our "upper room" where our congregation, The Church of the Advocate, would commemorate our Lord's Last Supper with other disciples. After dinner, we would bring basins and towels and wash one another's feet. I know some people do not like participating in this old rite. And yet, at the Church of the Advocate, we all participated! We were happy and grateful for the opportunity to follow Jesus's example.

I would like to focus on two words in the Vulgate (Latin) version of John's account: The first one appears in verse 15 and is the word *exemplum*: "I have given you an example." The second one appears outside of today's reading, in verse 34, and it is the word *mandatum*; it means "commandment" and gives origin to the expression "Maundy Thursday." Verse 34 reads: "A new commandment I give unto you, That ye love one another; as I have loved you, that ye also love one another."

We follow Jesus's *exemplum* with this simple act of humility and service: washing each other's feet. But Jesus's *mandatum* takes the *exemplum* to an entirely new dimension. The *mandatum* is not only about washing feet. It is about how we treat our loved ones day in and day out. It is about how we interact with neighbors and co-workers. It is about how we react when a friend or a stranger posts something that we don't like on Facebook. If you think about it, the *mandatum* encompasses our whole personal value system—for whom we vote, how we travel, and where we shop.

When the time comes for the foot washing, I'm always there, first in line, taking off my shoes and socks. This year, I had my feet washed and dried off by Deacon Dave; then Bob sat in Deacon Daves's chair, and I proceeded to wash and dry off Bob's feet. I couldn't help but think about all the pain I have had in my feet in the last three months. I did not have faith to believe that Dave's washing of my feet would heal me, yet during the washing I felt a profound connection with Deacon Dave, Bob, and the whole congregation. Silently, Jesus told me: "Hugo, I am not going to deliver you magically from your foot pain, but look—you are surrounded by loving people who care about all your ailments and all your pains."

—*Hugo Olaiz*

Saturday of the First Week in Lent

The Price He Paid

And there were also two other malefactors, led with him to be put to death. And when they were come to the place, which is called Calvary, there they crucified him, and the malefactors, one on the right hand, and the other on the left. Then said Jesus, Father, forgive them; for they know not what they do. And they parted his raiment, and cast lots. And the people stood beholding. And the rulers also with them derided him, saying, He saved others; let him save himself, if he be Christ, the chosen of God.

LUKE 23:32-35

I'd guess that connecting the cross with paying a price is a little uncomfortable for many Episcopalians. Some of this discomfort no doubt arises from a worthwhile attempt at distancing ourselves from those traditions that, at best, appear to reduce this complex mystery to a business transaction and, at worst, paint a picture of sadistic God granting pardon only upon receipt of sufficient human misery. At the same time, this discomfort may be traced back less laudably to an unfortunate Episcopal tendency to avoid talk of sin or our inability to save ourselves.

In either case—and I know my discomfort is a mixture of both—we ignore such language at our peril. That the work of the cross remains a mystery irreducible to the scriptural images that point toward it does not make any of those images inconsequential. The New Testament, from Matthew through Revelation, describes our salvation as involving redemption, ransoming, or purchase (see, for instance, Matthew 20:28, 1 Corinthians 6:20, Ephesians 1:7, 1 Peter 18-19, or Revelation 5:9). We can only ignore that this work has something in common with paying a price if we neglect large swaths of scripture.

As important as this image is, though, what are we supposed to do with it? Does not Christ accomplish on the cross precisely what we cannot do for ourselves? I propose that there is another price that Christ pays on the cross, not of our redemption but the price of his full humanity.

The affirmation that Christ is fully human is not merely an affirmation about him—it is also an affirmation about humanity. Christ, undistorted by sin, reveals true humanity to all of us whose humanity is distorted by sin. Christ reveals that the character of true humanity is love, an openness to what is outside of ourselves, an alignment with God's will and union with God. Aligned with God's will, true humanity calls us to recognize the dignity of our neighbors and work for their good as we remain open to relationship with them.

Sin-distorted humanity could never tolerate true humanity in its midst. Turned inward on itself, disconnected from God, its infinite source and goal, distorted humanity can only strive for self-perseveration through consumption, competition, oppression, objectification, and violence. To distorted humanity, the proclamation of a humanity open to the other for their own sake, to self-giving, to vulnerability is not only foolish and naïve—it is dangerous.

Crucifixion is the price Christ paid for his true humanity. This whole violent, humiliating, public spectacle went beyond pain or even killing—it meant to dehumanize, to objectify, to turn the victim into a symbol of incompetence, an object lesson for all those tempted to follow in their footsteps.

And yet, amid all the pain, mockery, and humiliation, Christ remains in control. True humanity proves more powerful than the violence and death brought to bear against him. He refuses to resign himself to admitting defeat. He refuses to call down heavenly armies to meet violence with violence, to play by the rules of distorted humanity. Instead, he calls for forgiveness. He remains open to the possibility of relationship to the very end on the cross.

Because Christ paid the price that none of us can pay, we can now follow him in the path of true humanity. Incorporated into Christ's death and resurrection in baptism, we can truly find openness to self-giving relationships with others. Secure in God's infinite life, we can reject the false promise of self-preservation through violence and domination. By following Christ's example, through having our humanity restored, we too may be called to pay a price, to experience resistance from the powers of sin and death thrashing about even in the midst of their defeat. But we stand firm on the hope that just as sin and death did not have the final say for Christ, so too will we who follow the path of Christ's life and death also follow him in his resurrection.

—*Chris Corbin*

LEARNS

Second Week in Lent

A DISCIPLE LEARNS

We follow Christ with our wills, but we can't get far without our minds. If I am making my life over by the pattern, I must know what he is like. I find I don't know. Searching the scriptures now has a point. To the eager searcher, the gospels fairly gleam with interest and surprise. Study the Master's life in the gospels. Commit sayings to memory. But remember, he isn't dead. Your partner is out in front, leading on. Take your cue from him: new truth, answers to questions. Never mind the psychology of it.

What does his Church teach? What is the Church's mission? The field? Who works there? And at what? Who pays for it? Plenty to learn here. And then our world. Has Christ a mind about slums, child labor, poverty, wealth, waste, unemployment, profits, standards, class strife, race clashes, injustice, war? Hard thinking needed here—and then action.

QUESTIONS: How much of my mental stock is truth and how much prejudice? After you STUDY a person or a people, which increases more: respect or dislike?

RESOLVE: This Lent, I will study a gospel, and some such book that tells of Jesus's life and history.

I love to learn. In fact, love of learning is a trait many Episcopalians have in common. Many people I have worshiped alongside in Episcopal churches have actively leaned into the more "academic" side of discipleship—coming to Bible studies and Sunday morning classes, for example. This impulse to learn is a good and holy thing because, as Jesus says in Matthew 22:37, we are to: "Love the Lord your God with all your heart, and with all your soul, and with all your mind." Learning more about our faith, tradition, and scripture can be an amazing way to stoke that curiosity for the unfathomable God who made the cosmos!

However, I sometimes wonder if Episcopalians neglect the "heart and soul" part of that commandment and think that the learning we do with our minds can substitute for other ways of knowing. In fact, there is a significant difference between knowing and wisdom in the biblical tradition. Knowledge is gathered through study, and wisdom is acquired through putting that knowledge into practice. For example, if we are walking down a road and read a sign that says, "Danger, the bridge is out ahead," we have all the knowledge we need to make an informed decision. But we are not truly wise if we keep walking. To fully integrate everything we learn about God through our mindful studies, we must feel them in our hearts and put them into practice in our lives.

A compelling way to practice this kind of wisdom learning is to read each scripture this week following the pathway of *lectio divina* or sacred reading. This ancient prayer style lets you read scripture with your whole heart, soul, and mind and encourages you to truly live what you read instead of just cognate it.

Lectio divina has four movements that can take as little or as long as you like:

1. *Lectio* (read): In this movement, you are invited to read the passage aloud and listen for a word or phrase that stands out. There is no need to ascribe any meaning to it yet; just sit and listen to the Word of God.

2. *Meditation*: Start by rereading the passage. In *lectio divina*, meditation means engaging with the scripture mentally. This time is our chance to think and learn. We can even research the word or phrase we were given today. This is a great time to read the daily meditation to see how others have thought about this passage and learn from their wisdom.

3. *Oratio* (pray): In this step, we turn away from simply using our minds and ask God how we might learn to be more like Christ today. As you read the passage for a third time, you are invited to ask the Holy Spirit to give you the grace to see your call in what you have read and learned today.

4. *Contemplation*: Finally, we are invited to enter the soul level of our prayer, where we surrender all the thoughts and worries of our lives and simply be with God. In this space, we can learn what God wants us to be aware of and gather energy to live wisely (not just learnedly) through our day.

—*Hillary Raining*

Monday of the Second Week in Lent

Jesus's Secret

In the mean his disciples prayed him, saying, Master, eat. But he said unto them, I have meat to eat that ye know not of. Therefore said the disciples one to another, Hath any man brought him ought to eat? Jesus saith unto them, My meat is to do the will of him that sent me, and to finish his work.

JOHN 4:31-34

As Christians, we learn Jesus's ways by reading and reflecting on the gospels. These are the stories that the Holy Spirit inspired the first followers of Jesus to preserve. By marinating ourselves daily in the stories of our savior's life and ministry, we discover more about how the God who is love lives out love in the messiness of actual human existence. Then, as we begin to pattern our lives from what we read, the lessons get woven into the fabric of our lives.

This is a much better practice than using the Bible on an as-needed basis. We are better served to know the Bible well before facing challenges, from a cancer diagnosis to friends

betraying us or a marriage unraveling. The Bible is not a troubleshooting guide.

I noticed that reading the Bible every day was the practice of people in my life who seemed to navigate problems best. When a prayed-up member of the Daughters of the King who reads the Bible each day runs into an issue, she has a strong foundation: "I am not sure how God has got this, but I know God does." Beyond this, years of running into bumps in life give one experience in seeing how God is faithful in such difficulties. This provides more reason to be confident that Jesus will not leave or forsake you.

A pattern of daily reading has long been the Episcopal Church's normative way of encountering scripture. Morning and Evening Prayer in the Book of Common Prayer were designed centuries ago, and the daily reading of scripture is part of the context of worship. *Forward Day by Day* was created to encourage daily reading of scripture.

With this brief commitment of time added to your morning routine or commute time, you steep your life in God's Word. What this will do for your outlook over time is revolutionary. Rather than encountering issues in life and running to the Bible for answers, you will immerse yourself in the Bible daily and live into the answers from that new outlook.

The daily readings will not always feel so essential to a particular day. Sometimes, you will read, and they are just words on a page. But if you continue with the practice, the Holy Spirit will bless your commitment, and you will discover days when it feels like a passage was written solely for you to read at that moment.

We see how scripture mattered in the life of our Savior. Jesus knows the texts in his bones, often bringing just the right quote from the Hebrew Bible into his preaching and teaching. In our reading for today, Jesus tells his followers that he is nourished by doing the will of God. As he says this, he has just encountered a Samaritan woman at a well at noon. She found the exchange so life-changing that she went to evangelize her village.

God has given our fleeting lives something enduring to which we can anchor. This is why the Disciples' Way teaches us to school our minds and hearts. When we integrate Jesus's life and teaching into our thinking, we are transformed in how we see the world. And when we put that faith in Jesus into practice, the lessons lead to further conversion.

I have experienced this in working on a Habitat for Humanity build. In taking the time to work alongside a neighbor as we create good, affordable housing, I also come to know my neighbors better. This leads me to a great concern for the needs in my community, which has me reading scripture with new eyes. In this way, the reading influences the way I live. This change of priority in my life influences my further study. Through this process, I encounter the Bible as God's living Word fashioned to speak to my heart each day as I seek to put love into action.

—*Frank Logue*

Tuesday of the Second Week in Lent

The Kingdom First

And seek not ye what ye shall eat, or what ye shall drink, neither be ye of doubtful mind. For all these things do the nations of the world seek after: and your Father knoweth that ye have need of these things. But rather seek ye the kingdom of God; and all these things shall be added unto you… For where your treasure is, there will your heart be also.

LUKE 12:29-31, 34

But rather seek ye the kingdom of God; and all these things shall be added unto you… Once upon a time, in a country far, far away, lived a queen who had ruled for a very long time. This queen had triplets, and as the years went by, she needed to decide which child would rule once she was gone. She wracked her brain, trying to devise ways to discern which one would be a good ruler and who would wear the crown after she was gone. After some time, she had three rooms built in the palace and gathered her children to her. She said to her children, "My years have been long, and my horizon is almost upon me. The time has come to decide which of you will wear the crown.

Before you are three rooms, identical in every way. Your task is simple. You have three days to fill your room, and the one who fills the room will become my heir." Excitedly, the children all ran off to decide how best to answer the challenge that was before them.

Three days later, the queen gathered with her children. In the first room, the child had spent three days gathering boulders and filling the room with large rocks. "Well done!" said the queen. "You have relied on your strength to fill the room, but there is still more that could be done." In the next room, the second child had painstakingly spent three days filling the room with sand. "Well done!" said the queen. "You have relied on your wisdom to fill the room, but there is still more that could be done."

Coming to the final room, the third child had spent three days feeding the poor of the city, planting crops with the farmers, and listening to the desires of the people. As the queen and the other two walked into the room, the third child walked over to a candle and, pausing in prayer, lit the wick and filled the room with light. "You shall be my heir!" declared the queen. "You have listened in love and shared the greatest gift of all, the light of hope."

We need hope. God knows we need hope.

Our lives are surrounded by so many occasions and opportunities to be of doubtful mind. Wars and rumors of war, natural disasters, and division dominate our social media. Families live with deep division and painful wounds. Gun violence plagues our urban centers and our rural regions. The list of difficulties is long and varied. In some ways, we have become comfortable with the way things are.

The same was true in Jesus's time. Injustice, oppression, and despair were the world into which he was born. Yet, the gloom of the world was pierced with the birthing cries of a child that promised hope.

Like the children in the story, we can engage with strength. We can, even for a time, apply wisdom, but hope is what carries us on and sees us through. Hope, no matter how bright or dim, points us toward the reign of God and grounds us in love. Hope is a powerful force that undergirds our faith with the foundation of love.

We modern followers of Jesus along the Way are not divorced from the world or removed from its worries. We engage with a broken world through the hope of the one who has walked in love. Our hope is in Jesus, not in the things we possess or the power we wield, but in the love we share, the love we receive, and the love we give. The kingdom of God is built on hope, and in Jesus, we see the hope of the world.

—*Deon K. Johnson*

Wednesday of the Second Week in Lent

Don't Be a Fool

The ground of a certain rich man brought forth plentifully: And he thought within himself, saying, What shall I do because I have no room where to bestow my fruits? And he said, This will I do: I will pull down my barns, and build greater; and there will I bestow all my fruits and my goods. And I will say to my soul, Soul, thou hast much goods laid up for many years; take thine ease, eat, drink, and be merry. But God said unto him, Thou fool, this night thy soul shall be required of thee: then whose shall those things be, which thou hast provided? So is he that layeth up treasure for himself, and is not rich toward God.

LUKE 12:16B-21

This parable seems aimed at America's consumer society where, if you ask how much someone is worth, it doesn't mean how generous, honest, or compassionate she is, but how much money she has. People are judged by their wealth, and many sacrifice everything else—family, friendship, health, virtue, peace of mind—for the big house on the hill set back from the road.

Jesus said more about the dangers of wealth than any other topic. So far as we know, Jesus possessed nothing apart from a robe. He had no place to lay his head (Matthew 8:20), and while many people welcomed him into their homes, he himself seems to have been homeless. "Do not store up for yourselves treasures on earth, where moth and rust consume and where thieves break in and steal; but store up for yourselves treasures in heaven, where neither moth nor rust consumes and where thieves do not break in and steal," Jesus taught (Matthew 6:19-20).

It's not that being rich is wrong, nor is being poor a virtue. Jesus didn't tell us to be destitute but "poor in spirit" (Matthew 5:3). Actual poverty can crush the human soul, and wealth, shared generously, can be a godsend to many. But wealth isn't often shared generously; usually, it seduces the possessor.

I remember an incident told to me by a friend in Alabama. She was a professional woman advancing in her firm and acquiring assets that marked her as a success. One morning, she talked to a client on her cellphone while pouring cereal and milk into a bowl for her daughter's breakfast. The daughter asked her mother to take her to the beach that day. The mother said she couldn't because she had an appointment with an important client. Her daughter said, "Mommy, when can I be a client?" Happily, in this case, Mommy rescheduled her appointment and took her little girl to the beach. I like to think that was a turning point for the mother, a moment when she became poor in spirit and decided some things were more important than the big house on the hill.

Then there was Thelma. The 75-year-old widow of a prominent West Virginia businessman, Thelma had the big house on the hill. She lived alone in her elegant, three-story English Tudor mansion with oriental rugs piled on hardwood floors, Ming vases on the sideboard, silk draperies, a box full of diamond pins and earrings, and enough sterling to open a silver shop. One night, robbers broke into her home, tied her to her bed, and stole everything. When I called on her the next day, I found Thelma in shock, disoriented, and confused.

Sometime later, when I called on her again, Thelma had undergone a remarkable transformation. She was composed and seemingly content, even happy. I saw inexpensive, rubber-backed rugs on her floors, mass-produced porcelain lamps, stainless steel flatware on the dining room table, and other items I had seen in the local K-Mart store.

"I've replaced everything," Thelma said matter-of-factly as if telling me she had just stepped out for the mail. "I suppose I would have been angry once. I'll miss those things, of course, because of the memories of my husband I associated with them. But it was just stuff. One doesn't have to sit in a Chippendale chair. One doesn't have to walk on Persian carpets. Food tastes just as good off plastic plates with stainless steel utensils. I'm alive; that's the important thing! And I must tell you I'm lucky to be alive because for the entire time, they had me tied up, I prayed at the top of my lungs for them. They threatened me if I didn't stop it, but I kept praying. Finally, they put a gag in my mouth!" Thelma smiled as she told me this.

It humbled me to listen to her. Here was someone accustomed to great wealth but genuinely poor in spirit. I shall never forget her.

—*Richard H. Schmidt*

Thursday of the Second Week in Lent

> # God and My Neighbor
>
> *And one of the scribes came, and having heard them reasoning together, and perceiving that he had answered them well, asked him, Which is the first commandment of all? And Jesus answered him, The first of all the commandments is, Hear, O Israel; The LORD our God is one Lord: And thou shalt love the Lord thy God with all thy heart, and with all thy soul, and with all thy mind, and with all thy strength: this is the first commandment. And the second is like, namely this, Thou shalt love thy neighbour as thyself.*
>
> MARK 12:28-31

Following Christ with our heart, mind, soul, and strength requires learning what it means to be a disciple. A disciple of Christ is one who follows the words and actions of Jesus Christ. This means there is no following, no discipleship, without asking questions. Sometimes, people of faith believe that it is wrong to have questions about faith or wrong to question God. However, experience shows that God can be described as the one who welcomes our questions and wants our engagement.

Spiritual questions, at their heart, lead us to a deeper understanding of God and our neighbor. In truth, our spiritual questions help us grow as disciples who understand the important connections between loving God and our fellow human beings. A disciple learns that to follow God is to be in right relationship with God and our neighbor.

Our gospel passage shows Jesus responding to one of the scribes. The scribe asks Jesus, "Which is the first commandment?" What question would you ask Jesus if the choice were yours? If you could ask Jesus Christ a question about God and your neighbor, what would that question be?

It is important to notice that Jesus answers the question asked of him. Sometimes, we overlook this important detail. It serves us well to remember and know that Jesus Christ does and will answer our questions. Jesus has an answer for you, your life, and all your concerns. In response to the scribe's question, Jesus responds with a most familiar response: "Hear, O Israel; the LORD our God is one Lord."

Lately, I have been paying attention to how ancient cultures looked at knowledge and how we have come to know anything. I discovered that for Greeks, the emphasis was on "seeing." For our Jewish brothers and sisters, the emphasis was on "hearing."

There is no love of God and neighbor without "hearing." We cannot love God unless we hear the very voice of God calling us into covenant, calling us into relationship, and calling us into Love. There is no loving of God without hearing God's call to our heart, mind, soul, and strength. Once we hear God, we can begin to love God.

We each need to remember that loving our neighbors requires listening to them. We see the breakdown, rejection, and failure of Christianity when we fail to hear our neighbors. We cannot love our neighbor without hearing their cries, questions, and desires. This has been the crime and the mortal sin of Christian missionaries. This has been the crime and the mortal sin of the church: refusing to hear and believing that other cultures, peoples, and ways of being have nothing worth hearing.

Hear, O Israel, the LORD our God is one Lord. This should make us think about the ways in which hearing makes us one with God. What do we hear about God that makes us more connected to God? What do we hear about God and our neighbor that makes us more willing to love with all our hearts? What do we hear from God when we get quiet and listen with the ears of the heart?

God and our neighbors become deeper desires of our loving response when we commit to hearing. May we hear the voice, presence, and needs of God and our neighbor as we continue our Lenten journey. Can we hear Jesus Christ calling us to be good news to the poor, telling prisoners that they are free and the blind they can see? Can we hear Jesus Christ calling us to love God and our neighbor?

—*Mark Francisco Bozzuti-Jones*

Friday of the Second Week in Lent

Related by Will

There came then his brethren and his mother, and, standing without, sent unto him, calling him. And the multitude sat about him, and they said unto him, Behold, thy mother and thy brethren without seek for thee. And he answered them, saying, Who is my mother, or my brethren? And he looked around about on them which sat about him, and said, Behold my mother and my brethren! For whosoever shall do the will of God, the same is my brother, and my sister, and mother.

MARK 3:31-35

My brother remembers the embarrassment I brought to him as I would greet him at the bus stop wearing pantyhose on my head, saying I was the evil villain KAOS from the *Get Smart* TV show. We have all felt embarrassed by family members. In the Gospel of Mark, Jesus's family is embarrassed by the scene he is causing. His healings and exorcisms are prompting people to spread rumors about Jesus. Eventually, his family has had enough of the rumors and suggestions, and they question Jesus. They worry he has lost his mind.

In Jesus's day, the family was everything. You lived with your family, worked with your family, and received honor and shame from your family. That is why Jesus's teaching is shocking. It rejects family as an identity marker.

Jesus is reinterpreting the definition of family. We often use familial language to talk about our church community, and the language is so comfortable to us that we miss how shocking it was to those in Nazareth who heard Jesus's words.

One of the challenges in a culture heavily formed by Christian beliefs and virtues is that we can easily assume our identities and preferences are Christian. Anytime we replace our relationship with Jesus for other identity markers like nationality, political party, or social class, we are no longer learning our identity from our savior. Jesus challenges our allegiances and asks us to follow him. In baptism, we reject the powers and principalities of this world that draw us from the way of Jesus and commit ourselves to follow him.

Baptized into Jesus's death and resurrection is our core identity. At each baptism, we pray that those baptized may have a discerning and inquiring heart. Too often, we replace a relationship with Jesus with information about Jesus. As long as learning remains a matter of the head, we keep Jesus at bay. We protect ourselves from allowing God to transform and change our lives. Learning is not just an academic endeavor but a matter of the heart, guided by the Spirit.

In the Easter stories, Jesus is found in Word, Table, and Community (our family). Encountering Jesus by reading and reflecting on scripture, regularly receiving communion, and living life with others who have committed their lives to follow Jesus provides a pattern of learning that will challenge every other notion of identity we have.

—*Everett Lees*

Saturday of the Second Week in Lent

You Do It to Him

For I was an hungered, and ye gave me meat: I was thirsty, and ye gave me drink: I was a stranger, and ye took me in: Naked, and ye clothed me: I was sick, and ye visited me: I was in prison, and ye came unto me. Then shall the righteous answer him, saying, Lord, when saw we thee an hungered, and fed thee? or thirsty, and gave thee drink? When saw we thee a stranger, and took thee in? or naked, and clothed thee? Or when saw we thee sick, or in prison, and came unto thee? And the King shall answer and say unto them, Verily I say unto you, Inasmuch as ye have done it unto one of the least of these my brethren, ye have done it unto me.

MATTHEW 25:35-40

I have a theory about the problem with organized religion. We spend a lot of time, effort, and money on things that don't matter—and very little of our attention on the things that matter. We stage awesome church services, but we often struggle when the time comes to feed the hungry, visit the sick, and welcome the stranger.

Jesus knows this, and that is why his teachings can seem harsh. We perform elaborate rituals, display fancy trappings, and play and sing fancy music, but sometimes, we "neglect the weightier matters of the law," or, to put it more bluntly, we "strain out a gnat but swallow a camel" (Matthew 23:22-24).

I see how Jesus's followers attempt to correct the course in the gospels and in the whole New Testament. Early Christians shared everything they had (Acts 2:44-46), took care of the widows (Acts 6:1-7), and sent support to the impoverished Christians of Jerusalem (1 Corinthians 16:1-4). James's Epistle goes so far as to offer this radical definition of pure religion: "to care for orphans and widows in their distress, and to keep oneself unstained by the world" (1:27). And I see a similar impulse in Hebrews: after a long theological reflection about how "it is impossible for the blood of bulls and goats to take away sins" (10:4), the author urges us to refocus on Jesus (12:2). "Do not neglect to do good and to share what you have," the author concludes, "for such sacrifices are pleasing to God" (13:16).

By the fourth century, some churches had grown very rich and had forgotten that "pure religion" preached by James. John Chrysostom issued one of the most compelling indictments against the church of his day. "For what is the profit, when Christ's table indeed is full of golden cups, but he perishes with hunger?" Chrysostom asked in one of his homilies. "First fill him, being an hungered, and then abundantly deck his table also."

Our challenge as Christians is to be constantly vigilant and not confuse pure religion with its many trappings. When we dress the altar, let it remind us to clothe the naked. When we share the peace, let it remind us to welcome the stranger. When we partake of the bread and the wine, let us recommit our lives to feeding the hungry and giving drink to the thirsty.

—*Hugo Olaiz*

PRAYS

Third Week in Lent

A DISCIPLE PRAYS

We humans have a homing instinct. Don't believe those who say you are caged in fast behind your five senses. You have wings. The door is open. It is your power to pray. Of course, if God is only an abstraction, a blind force, a system of morals, then you have nowhere to go. But God is Our Father: we are God's children. Prayer is too deep to prattle about. Use it, and you will know.

Study the Father and Son story in Luke 15 as a clue to prayer. It's nearly all Father: home, inheritance, following love, recall, forgiveness, welcome, joyful company. All the son does is to come to himself and come home, just as he is. Yes, prayer has difficulties. But what if the boy had never acted on, "I will arise and go to my Father"? Even so, he expected to be a slave—not to be met halfway as a son. Put bluntly: prayer is getting home to Our Father, listening, looking, getting the viewpoint—the joy of God's company.

SUGGESTIONS: God loves to hear you as a parent to a child. Use little prayers all day long—your own natural words. Spend time full of thanks, realizing something of Our Father's great goodness—yourself—and your worries forgotten. Pray little for yourself and much for others.

During the liturgy for Ash Wednesday, the congregation is invited to the observance of a holy Lent, with a list of ways to respond to that invitation and grow in faith during this season (see page 265 in the Book of Common Prayer for that invitation.) One of the ways to grow is through a commitment to prayer, which is the focus for this coming week.

As we think about prayer as an expression of discipleship, we might begin by looking at what Jesus taught about prayer. One of his most powerful teaching tools was his example. It's remarkable how much time Jesus spent in prayer. Again and again, we find him going off by himself to pray, capped by his choice to pray by himself in the Garden of Gethsemane. In my tendency toward clergy over-functioning, I often ask, "How did he have time to do that? He only had three years to change the course of history!" The fact that our Lord and Savior made time to deepen his relationship with the one he called Father tells us that it matters. Disciples since have come to know that. Martin Luther used to spend more than three hours a day in prayer. He was asked how he had time to do that in his busy schedule of reforming Europe. He simply said he was too busy not to pray.

When Jesus's disciples asked to be taught about prayer, he gave them the Lord's prayer, a mark of their identity as a community. He established a tradition that exists today; every liturgy in our prayer book contains this simple prayer. The Lord's Prayer has all we need to guide us in a prayer life, including a beginning that marks right relationship with the one we call Father. The prayer begins by approaching our Father in heaven, asking that God's name be hallowed. Among other things, that means that our prayer life starts with a focus on God and not ourselves.

That's why our prayers include both praise and thanksgiving. We praise as we see our lives unfolding in the presence of a living God who has created all things. We set our hearts in right attention with that praise. And, in our prayers, we aim for an attitude of gratitude, noting what Meister Eckhard said about prayer: the only word we need to know in prayer is thanks.

We pray to set ourselves in right relationship to God, confessing ways we have fallen short of living into that relationship and admitting we have not loved God with our whole being. We have not loved our neighbor as self. Those shortcomings are true every day of my life. Disciples know that. So that we might draw closer to God, we begin our private and corporate prayer time with confession.

After that, we bring the intercessions, the supplications on our heart, those things we wish to lift before God, having recognized that God meets us not only with the power that created the universe but also with the love from which we can never be separated. This is not envisioning God as a celestial valet or Santa Claus. This is not telling God what to do. But as we each carry concerns in our hearts for the needs of those around us, we lift them to the Lord.

In all of this, we envision discipleship as the relationship with God; we find prayer life enriched as we listen. We've found that those whose spiritual life is most at the center of their life spend the most time in contemplative reflection, in silence.

Those of us in church can sometimes make prayer more complicated than it needs to be. We need not pray with the eloquence of the Book of Common Prayer. The author Anne Lamott says we really only need to know three words in prayer: thanks, help, and wow.

May your prayer life this Lenten season grow and deepen your discipleship as you follow the one who taught his disciples to pray, and who teaches us still.

—Jay Sidebotham

Monday of the Third Week in Lent

The Lord's Prayer

And it came to pass, that, as he was praying in a certain place, when he ceased, one of his disciples said unto him, Lord, teach us to pray, as John also taught his disciples. And he said unto them, When ye pray, say, Our Father which art in heaven, Hallowed be thy name. Thy kingdom come, Thy will be done, as in heaven, so in earth. Give us day by day our daily bread. And forgive us our sins; for we also forgive every one that is indebted to us. And lead us not into temptation; but deliver us from evil.

LUKE 11:1-4

I once had a friend who would only call if she needed something. She treated all of us in our friend group that way. Whenever she needed something from us, she'd call.

However, she never reciprocated. Whenever we attempted to share our struggles, she hijacked the conversation to talk about herself.

Eventually, I put her name on my phone as "Do Not Answer" because it's hard to be in a friendship with someone who only takes and takes and takes.

Many have a similar attitude toward prayer, where all we do is ask God for things instead of being in conversation—and listening. It's as if God and prayer are the "break in case of emergency" last resort when we desperately need God's help to bail us out.

This attitude may explain why it's hard to understand what Paul means when he says, "Pray without ceasing." If our prayers are nothing more than wish lists, we have limited the power of prayer and what it does for our souls. In essence, we become my college friend known as "Do Not Answer."

Asking God for something and/or bartering with God is a part of praying; it is not the only thing about praying. A pastor told me that breathing is to our lungs as prayer is to our souls. Prayer is more of an attitude — a posture in life. And it isn't limited to only words.

Prayer is a form of communication with God. It is how we stay connected to God's spirit.

In prayer, we commune with God. We thank God. We bless God. We adore God. We praise God. We confess to God. And we ask God for help.

Prayer is not a transaction. It's not some negotiating tactic or ploy. Prayer is not an attempt to change God's mind but to allow God to change our minds about the world before us. American theologian and Jesuit priest Gregory Boyle once said, "The only problem prayer solves is you." Prayer is not about outcome but about being in communion with our Creator, allowing God to sustain us.

When we met our (then foster) son, we were told that he only knew five "words" at age three. That first year, I yearned to talk to and communicate with him. Over the years, his vocabulary has expanded, and now, at the age of 13, we can have small conversations (my son is on the autism spectrum). There's no wrong way for my son to communicate with us. I don't expect him to use SAT vocabulary words when speaking with us—nor would I want him to. I just want him to continue talking to us—as he is.

I think that goes for God, too. Be yourself. Use your words. Pray as you can, and don't pray as you can't.

Simply pray.

—*Joseph Yoo*

Tuesday of the Third Week in Lent

Tell Your Father

And I say unto you, Ask, and it shall be given you; seek, and ye shall find; knock, and it shall be opened unto you. For every one that asketh receiveth; and he that seeketh findeth; and to him that knocketh it shall be opened. If a son shall ask bread of any of you that is a father, will he give him a stone? ... If ye, then, being evil, know how to give good gifts unto your children: how much more shall your heavenly Father give the Holy Spirit to them that ask him?

LUKE 11:9-11,13

Bargaining with God will get you nowhere. God is God, and we are human. We often try to curate our communication, believing that if we ask God in just the right way, we'll get exactly what we want. How many of us do this regularly? Be warned: this could easily have disastrous consequences, including the loss of our faith!

Occasionally, I've heard people say they have lost their faith because God did not give them what they wanted when they prayed. This perceived "non-action" of God has caused individuals to doubt themselves—and doubt God. Some question their worthiness to be loved by God. Others embark on desperate behaviors of self-harm because they have convinced themselves that they no longer have the capacity or the ability to communicate to God in prayer. Nothing could be further from the truth!

As a child, I sincerely believed God would act if my faith were strong enough. Over and over, I would pray for things I wanted, only to be disappointed that they did not happen as I had hoped. At times, my doubts surged, but the Living God had other things in mind for me. This type of prayer, this bargaining with God, continued in a whole host of ways, most especially when I was praying to get a good grade, negotiating in prayer that the popular kids in school would like me, or even that my earnings in a summer job would be enough to pay for some big purchase. These practices continued in my early adulthood. Some of these prayers were superficial, while others were heartfelt. This curated prayer regimen had me praying for good results from a diet and exercise program before a trip to the beach and negotiating in prayer how God would love me if I came out of the closet in an authentic way.

The problem with these types of prayers was that, deep down, I did not believe that God's purposes for me were always good. The truth is that God did answer my prayers—in the same manner that God answers yours and will continue to do so. As disciples of Jesus, we are called to grow up and refine our prayers in the purest way possible, but not so that we can say the right words! God wants our hearts, our longings, our desires. God wants our whole, raw, unedited selves to approach God's throne of grace in prayer. God honestly does not care about word choice. God wants our hearts and all the spectrum of our emotions that we experience. Through prayer, God promises to fill our hearts with love.

The practice of prayer takes each disciple on a journey of a lifetime. With the exception of Jesus, no one formulates the perfect prayer, and this is perfectly okay. God accepts our prayers in whatever form they are offered, and God always answers prayer by giving us something we truly need. Praying means asking, seeking, and knocking, which Jesus says will lead us to not only what we need but also an abundant portion of the Holy Spirit, which will lead us into all truth.

Don't negotiate with God. Instead, be real. There is no reason to bargain in prayer. God wants to hear what you really want, on every level, in every way you can offer your prayer. In turn, we need to expect that we will receive a response, an abundant and generous response given specifically to us from the purest source of love imaginable.

— *Troy Mendez*

Wednesday of the Third Week in Lent

Turn Worry to Thanks

Be careful for nothing; but in every thing by prayer and supplication with thanksgiving let your requests be made known unto God. And the peace of God, which passeth all understanding, shall keep your hearts and minds through Christ Jesus. Finally, brethren, whatsoever things are true, whatsoever things are honest, whatsoever things are just, whatsoever things are pure, whatsoever things are lovely, whatsoever things are of good report; if there be any virtue, and if there by any praise, think on these things.

PHILIPPIANS 4:6-8

My grandfather turned worrying into a world-class event. As a child, I remember loading into the family car and driving the hour and a half to see my grandparents. Nine times out of ten, as we turned down their street and made the final approach to the house, there he was…pacing the driveway. He had been there for 30 minutes at least. This was in the days before cell phones and instant communication, and he had probably been worrying all day. Was the highway safe? What if the car had a breakdown? I imagine all his pacing wore a groove into the pavement as he conjured all sorts of what-ifs. And, knowing my grandfather, he said some prayers too. As we pulled into the driveway, his worries melted into joy as he performed a quick head count of his loved ones and smiled his famous crooked grin.

In the New Revised Standard Version of these verses from Philippians, the passage begins, "Do not be anxious about anything." Be careful for nothing. The message is all about being grounded in a life of prayer. Prayer certainly won't take away all the worries of this world, but it can be a balm for our souls.

At various times in my life, I have experienced uncertainty. You probably have, too, when discerning possible job transitions, navigating health challenges, or worrying about loved ones. In these situations, we are not in control and must choose to let go while trusting God. When living in these in-between times, it is essential that we carve out a regular, daily prayer routine. In the space in which we listen to God, we will find God's peace.

I like to think of my grandfather as a mystic on the move. He didn't sit still much. But I know he started each day with a cup of coffee and his well-worn Bible. He prayed, and he listened to God, and he kept on listening to God as he paced the driveway or typed out letters to loved ones or visited friends who were having a tough time.

Some of us are more prone to worry and anxiety. Several people who are very dear to me struggle with anxiety. When I'm in the midst of worry, I think of the life of Saint Julian of Norwich. She was a mystic in the fourteenth century who wrote vividly about her visions of Jesus.

As a young woman, Julian fell gravely ill, and everyone believed she would die. Those around her prepared for her death, and Last Rites were said, but then something happened. Maybe it was a near-death experience or a holy vision, but Julian experienced 15 revelations. In one of the revelations, Jesus said to her: "All shall be well, and all shall be well, and all manner of things shall be well."

May your worries turn to prayers. And may you remember this revelation from Julian, that in Christ, there is peace that passeth all understanding.

—*Kate E. Wesch*

Thursday of the Third Week in Lent

Prayer in Crisis

And he went forward a little, and fell on the ground, and prayed that, if it were possible, the hour might pass from him. And he said, Abba, Father, all things are possible unto thee; take away this cup from me: nevertheless not what I will, but what thou wilt. And he cometh, and findeth them sleeping, and saith unto Peter, Simon, sleepest thou? couldest not thou watch one hour? Watch ye and pray, lest ye enter into temptation. The spirit truly is ready, but the flesh is weak.

MARK 14:35-38

My journey into the Episcopal Church happened in no small part because of our language of prayer. Although I was initially attracted to a particular liturgical style of praying, it was the prayers themselves that formed me over several years, even in congregations with dramatically different aesthetic and liturgical sensibilities. I came to realize that my language of prayer and worship was that of the Book of Common Prayer.

As much as I have appreciated being formed by the prayer book, I don't have unreserved praise for everything in it. I wrestled with one prayer in particular for quite some time: a collect said by the celebrant at the end of the Prayers of the People in Rite II. I struggled with the line: "Help us to ask only what accords with your will."

This phase may seem a rather odd one to get tripped up on. After all, Jesus teaches us to pray, "Thy will be done." And yet, for me, at least, there can sometimes seem like a vast chasm between asking that God's will be done in the abstract and ensuring that my particular petitions align with God's will. So often, we don't know exactly what God's will is. Are we meant to hold back in prayer, only to bring those desires that we can be assured receive the divine seal of approval? How many people have been held back from a more intimate relationship with God for fear of their unworthiness? How many people have pulled back from uttering what is on their hearts out of embarrassment at being insufficiently holy?

Christ's own prayer in Gethsemane illuminates a path forward for us. Jesus, in his humanity, understandably wants to avoid the prolonged torture and agonizing death awaiting him, and so he implores his Father to spare him this fate if it is at all possible. But, in the end, Christ affirms his surrender to his Father's will. He submits to undergo whatever is necessary for the fulfillment of God's plan, even unto death on a cross.

This scene has proved incredibly generative for theologians speculating on Christ's human and divine natures. However interesting such speculation may be, debating about how much Christ knew, how he knew it, or even what this says about the trinitarian life is somewhat beside the point. Christ's prayer teaches us as his disciples that there is no request we need to hold back in prayer. If even Christ could ask for something in prayer that had the potential to be out of alignment with God's purposes, then we should be emboldened to bring whatever desires we have before God. And, at the same time, we must also follow Jesus's example by framing all our requests with "nevertheless, not what I will, but what thou wilt." We must be prepared for our petitions and intercessions to be opportunities for revelation, chances to learn where our wills are out of alignment with God's.

Christ's prayer in Gethsemane allows us to see the collect from the Prayers of the People in a new light. Asking for help to pray only what accords with God's will does not exclude offering in prayer what is on our hearts. In the end, such prayer can be God's means of helping us discern God's will and, if we are open to it, help our future prayers align more closely with that will.

—Chris Corbin

Friday of the Third Week in Lent

Make Prayer Real

And when thou prayest, thou shalt not be as the hypocrites are: for they love to pray standing in the synagogues and in the corners of the streets, that they may be seen of men. Verily I say unto you, They have their reward. But thou, when thou prayest, enter into thy closet, and when thou hast shut thy door, pray to thy Father which is in secret; and thy Father which seeth is secret shall reward thee openly.

MATTHEW 6:5-6

Years ago, I attended a conference on housing. One of our speakers was a government official in charge of public housing in his state. He spoke for more than an hour, reciting well-known facts as if they were stunning new insights on his part. Most of us quickly concluded that he was a lightweight and became annoyed at what seemed a waste of our time. Finally, during the question-and-answer time following his address, I raised my hand and said, "Sir, as a government functionary, would you say..." I never finished my question because the room burst into raucous laughter. Of course, I apologized, saying I hadn't meant those words the way they had sounded, that they had come out wrong. But I had meant them exactly as they had sounded; they had come out just as I had intended. I knew I'd get a big laugh at the speaker's expense and come across as sharp-witted and clever. I'd be the center of attention.

Seeking to be the center of attention is tricky. One doesn't want to be obvious about it. Pray on a street corner? Certainly not! I would never do that. Not only does Jesus explicitly censure people who pray on street corners, but this would be a clear attempt to attract attention to me. I want to be the center of attention, but I also want to appear humble-—not necessarily to be humble, just to appear humble.

For all my adult life, I've been a preacher, and I've sometimes wondered why I chose this profession years ago. The psychologist who interviewed me when I started in this ministry asked about my motivation. I remember giving an answer I believed was true and apparently satisfied him. But were there other motivations I wasn't aware of? I liked the thought of standing up every week before a group of people who would listen (or pretend to listen) to every word I said. I still do. Part of me wants people to say in response to one of my sermons, "What a great God!" But another part of me wants them to say, "What a great preacher!"

These two verses from the Sermon on the Mount are about more than grabbing the spotlight. They are about prayer. And the first thing to note is that Jesus talks about when his disciples pray, not if they pray. Prayer is an essential part of following Jesus. The question is not whether we pray but where, when, and how.

Jesus says to go into our closet, which I take to mean any private place. That's important because public prayer easily becomes a performance. I know this from having prayed at many a public event. In the back of my mind is always the question of how my words will be received—not by God but by the people in the room. It sometimes is more about me than about God.

There are many ways to pray: meditating on a scripture verse, singing, silent prayer, or using a rosary, prayer book, or icon. What is helpful for one person may not be right for the next person, and what is best for you today may not be best for you tomorrow. The key thing is that your prayer is about God, not about you. It is okay to pray for our concerns and needs. We are told to do that (Philippians 4:6), but the main reason we pray is to open our hearts to receive God's love. As Scottish evangelist Oswald Chambers said, "Prayer is getting into perfect communion with God."

In the words of a fourteenth-century hymn, "Come down, O love divine, seek thou this soul of mine, and visit it with thine own ardor glowing. O Comforter, draw near, within my heart appear, and kindle it, thy holy flame bestowing."

—Richard H. Schmidt

Saturday of the Third Week in Lent

God Prays in Us

Likewise the Spirit also helpeth our infirmities; for we know not what we should pray for as we ought; but the Spirit itself maketh intercession for us with groanings which cannot be uttered. And he that searcheth the hearts knoweth what is the mind of the Spirit, because he maketh intercession for the saints according to the will of God. And we know that all things work together for good to them that love God.

ROMANS 8:26-28A

I confess: I struggle with prayer. Don't get me wrong. I pray. And I have my share of testimonies about the power of prayer in my life and the lives of others. In fact, if there were one thing I could give to people who live without faith and find themselves in the midst of life's struggles, it would be prayer. But an honest description of my prayer life—at least when it comes to prayers about my struggles—is that when all else fails, I pray.

When I finally get to prayer, I always wonder why I didn't get there much sooner. I'm better about praying for others, both because they ask me to, and I like to try to do things that people ask me to do, and also because it is often the best way I know to respond when someone is suffering.

Paul suggests that all we need to do is give ourselves to prayer, and the Spirit will do most of the work. We don't need to tie ourselves in knots, formulate the perfect prayer, or find the most beautiful words. We don't need to worry that God will misunderstand us or that our errors and omissions will confuse God or lead to poorly answered prayers.

Paul also suggests that a lot of our prayers should be about other people. When the Spirit does our praying for us, it seems the Spirit mostly talks about the saints, that is, the other people who are also making their way along this sacred journey of life. Being sincerely prayed for is one of the most lovely things— perhaps a little uncomfortable for us introverts when it happens out loud—a bit like being wrapped in a warm blanket we didn't quite realize how much we needed.

Even so, prayer is embarrassing. In a secular world, there may be no part of the life of faith that seems quite as wacky to those outside our faith communities. If everyone you know goes to church, maybe get out more. If not, you probably know what I mean. People struggle to understand what we think we're doing with all this prayer. Fixing things? Calling down miracles? Avoiding responsibility? Spiritualizing the material? Talking to voices only we can hear?

Going back to the beginning of our text today, it turns out that being a little upside down and backward about prayer is expected. It is one of our infirmities, apparently. Thank God the

Spirit has taken notice and decided that we're not to be left alone in so important an arena of life and faith.

Our part of prayer seems to be drawing near enough to one another that the Spirit can get a good signal. The Spirit will then do her part, filling our hearts with intercession for one another's joys and sorrows. We need only bring the intention and the care for one another. What is revealed is one of the great comforting lines in scripture: that all things work together for good in those who love God.

—*Anna Olson*

SERVES

Fourth Week in Lent

A DISCIPLE SERVES

Well, we know the word SERVE. It conjures up power plants, telephones, street cars, railways, farms, mills, restaurants, mines, mails: all the trades, all professions. Without these servants, we should choke, freeze, starve, and die. Somewhere you have your part. Keep it up. Make it finer, gladder, more honest—a thing done to friends and God. Beyond the payroll you can serve. God is calling you through this Forward Movement to work for Him: in the home, in the community, and in the Church. You are to be Christ's agent, Christ's servant—a friend to someone, to many. Let God reign in this world. People must have a better life: work, food, decent homes, justice, peace, friendship, and relief from slavery, disease, ignorance, and sin. They must have God.

Here is service for the disciple and the Church. Work it out! Joy in it and pay for it as Christ did! Let God say one day, "Well done."

PRAY: O God, add me to your labor force.

AFFIRM: My work is in front of me. I will find it and do it.

DO THIS: Tackle duty first, no matter how ordinary or simple. Watch for a chance to serve. Have the pluck to do it. Serve through the Church. If you see no opening, ask your rector.

I love to host dinner parties. It's not just about good food and games but about creating a spiritual and relational space for connection and love. As much as I love hosting, I admit that it is hard work. The dinner party begins long before the first guests arrive, with the idea of the dinner party. After deciding to host a dinner party, several other decisions must be made in short order: who do we invite? What do we serve? How will we keep everyone entertained? Even once we've made these decisions, we must make many more decisions and complete many more tasks up to, during, and after the dinner party.

In all my years of hosting dinner parties, there is always a moment when I wonder if it is worth the effort. This usually happens when the first guests arrive as I'm putting the finishing touches on dinner, and I ask myself whether it would be easier to meet for dinner at a local restaurant. And yet, at the end of the night, as my husband and I put away the leftovers, load the dishwasher, and wipe down the counters, I always feel that the gathering was worth it. Invariably, I have learned something new about a friend, offered helpful connections, or created space for someone to experience love and care.

Christians serve. It is what we do. Despite the alluring gravitational pull of so much modern spirituality that seems to put us in the middle of everything, Christianity is primarily about serving others. Three of the four gospels record Jesus telling his disciples, "The Son of Man came not to be served but to serve, and to give his life a ransom for many." Jesus's life is defined by how much he could give himself away for the sake of others.

Too often, Christians are not known for this selflessness. Instead, much of the modern narrative about Christianity seems to center on how much space Christians want to take up in the world. My love of dinner parties has taught me that service's true nature is hospitality, allowing the other to show up. A mystical Jewish doctrine called *Tzimtzum*, first articulated by a sixteenth-century rabbi, captures divine hospitality perfectly. It says that God's glory filled the universe so thoroughly that it was impossible to create anything because there was no room. To create, God contracted to create a negative space—a space that was not God. There are similarities between this mystical doctrine and Paul's hymn in Philippians 2:6-8, where he writes that Jesus "who, though he was in the form of God, did not regard equality with God as something to be exploited, but emptied himself, taking the form of a slave, being born in human likeness. And being found in human form, he humbled himself and became obedient to the point of death— even death on a cross." Divine service is about emptying one's self for the sake of others.

Charity is one of the common themes and practices associated with the Lenten season. As we consider the nature of divine service—hospitality—it is worth thinking about what space we are creating within ourselves, our communities, and our world through our service. What becomes possible that was previously regarded as impossible? What identities and experiences are raised and granted dignity that were previously ignored and derided? We are the sacrament of Christ's ongoing presence in the world, called to do what he did: serve the poor and marginalized, forge connections and relationships, and heal harm and brokenness. This requires that we learn to make space for others and, in doing so, learn to make space for God.

—*Marcus George Halley*

Monday in the Fourth Week of Lent

You Serve Christ

And whatsoever ye do in word or deed, do all in the name of the Lord Jesus, giving thanks to God and the Father by him…. And whatsoever ye do, do it heartily, as to the Lord, and not unto men… for ye serve the Lord Christ.

COLOSSIANS 3:17, 23, 24B

Whosoever will be great among you, let him be your minister; and whosoever will be chief among you, let him be your servant: even as the Son of man came not to be ministered unto, but to minister, and to give his life a ransom for many.

MATTHEW 20:26B-28

One of the most intimate and beautiful aspects of serving God in the church is the people you meet. In the kingdom of God, relationship is primary, and building one another up in the body of Christ is part of our mandate as baptized Christians. I have served God and the church for two decades, and in that time, I have gotten to know so many wonderful human beings.

Today, I want to tell you about a man named Caleb, who died last year. Caleb was a walking heart in this world and is deeply missed. His life and witness spanned nearly a century, and he almost always had a smile on his face and a twinkle in his bright blue eyes.

Every single person I have met who also knew Caleb says, "He was my favorite." And indeed, he was my favorite, too. Why? What made this man so special? I didn't have the pleasure of meeting Caleb until he was already in his late 90s, and I began regularly visiting the local retirement home. He had lived in this retirement community for many years, having moved in long ago when his wife was sick. She died not long after they arrived, and Caleb had gone on to forge many deep friendships with residents and staff alike.

Even in a weakened physical state at the end of his life, it was clear Caleb was a leader who led from his heart. Caleb was always delighted to see you, regardless of who you were. He greeted each person—family, friend, therapist, caregiver, priest—with the same enthusiasm and focused attention. When you were talking with Caleb, he really listened, and you could tell he cared. He made each person feel as if you were his favorite, too.

We live in a small, rural community. The other day, I was getting my hair cut at the local salon when the stylist said, "Did you hear that Caleb died? He was my favorite."

"How did you know Caleb?" I asked.

I learned that Stacie used to work at the retirement home and was part of the team that offered programming and events for the residents. Some years ago, when Caleb's wife was sick, Stacie threw a mid-week party for the residents, a Root Beer Float Party. Stacie knew Caleb was looking forward to it, but when the time came, his wife fell ill, and they spent the afternoon at the emergency room instead.

The next day, Stacie made a perfect float with the whipped cream coiled just so and a cherry on top. She hand-delivered the float to Caleb's apartment, where he met her at the door with a big smile and a twinkle in his eyes. He promptly burst into tears. As he took a sip of the float, he told Stacie that he hadn't tasted a root beer float since he was a child, and her kindness meant the world to her.

When I think about servant leadership, I think about people like Caleb and Stacie. They are flexible, empathetic, generous, and kind. They listen deeply and respond to the image of Christ in others. Caleb was a lifelong leader, motivated by his deep and abiding faith in Jesus Christ and his genuine love of people. When I think about the kinds of leaders I want to follow, I think of Caleb. When I pray about the type of leader I want to be, I think about these tremendous examples I have witnessed of love, sharing of power, and always making others feel as if I am their favorite.

This type of leadership goes beyond "do unto others as you would have them do unto you." Servant leadership looks into the soul of another and celebrates the image of Christ that they bear.

—Kate E. Wesch

Tuesday in the Fourth Week of Lent

And So Serve Others

Owe no man anything, but to love one another: for he that loveth another hath fulfilled the law.... Love worketh no ill to his neighbor: therefore love is the fulfilling of the law.

ROMANS 13:8,10

Bear ye one another's burdens, and so fulfil the law of Christ.

GALATIANS 6:2

We then that are strong ought to bear the infirmities of the weak, and not to please ourselves.

ROMANS 15:1

The introduction to this week in the original devotional takes us back to a time when our culture may have had a broader and less individualistic view of service. The forms of service it describes are pretty mundane, just regular people "doing our jobs." Our current era, with its emphasis on fame and popularity, aspirations to be influencers, and college applications demanding to know how each child will make a unique and stunning contribution to society, doesn't have so much glory or even room for the grind of regular service. Meetings, cleaning kitchens, knitting one row after another, chopping onions, washing clothes, making coffee, counting the plate offering… there are a lot of little forms of service that make up the whole that we treasure.

As I have gotten older and more conscious of how many pieces go into the lives and communities I am a part of, I have become ridiculously grateful for the small things, the steadiness of the contributions of people who will never get more than a few "likes" for all that they do. When someone brings flowers to put on the table, remembers birthdays with a hand-signed card, or makes sure there is toilet paper in all the restrooms, I find my burdens lightened just by the sheer beauty of their offering.

It was a long time before I learned to ask for help. I thought that I should try to bear all my burdens before asking anyone else to get involved. I've come to see that something miraculous comes about when burdens are shared and blessings are multiplied. We are meant to do this life together, it seems. There is joy in carrying other people's burdens that I often fail to find in the weight of my own. There is joy in the receiving of love always, in someone else's act of noticing that I am heavy-laden, and in their willingness to help.

In the letter to the Galatians, Paul suggests that it is better that we pass the burdens around than manage them on our own. He relates the sharing of burdens to the basic work of building Christian community according to the fruits of the Spirit. His instructions come at the end of a rather fierce letter in which he mostly scolds the Galatians for the many ways they have strayed from the teachings of the Gospel. But at the end, he turns to a gentler tone, reminding them that there is always a way forward through the love of God and neighbor.

"Love worketh no ill to his neighbor." The readings for today remind us that love is not about trying to unmake and remake one another. Just as God comes to me, "Just as I Am," in the words of the beloved hymn, I am to take my neighbor as he or she or they are and serve them as I find them. The call to serve is not a call to fix, reshape, teach, or admonish. We are called to draw close to one another, loving, being, and delighting in another person God has made.

—*Anna Olson*

Wednesday in the Fourth Week of Lent

The Beatitudes

Blessed are the poor in spirit: for theirs is the kingdom of heaven. Blessed are they that mourn: for they shall be comforted. Blessed are the meek: for they shall inherit the earth. Blessed are they which do hunger and thirst after righteousness: for they shall be filled. Blessed are the merciful: for they shall obtain mercy. Blessed are the pure in heart: for they shall see God. Blessed are the peacemakers: for they shall be called the children of God.

MATTHEW 5:3-9

In N.T. Wright's book, *Matthew for Everyone*, he uses the movie *The Right Stuff* to illustrate how God's kingdom works. The film chronicles the development of the US space program and the efforts of pilots to fly beyond the sound barrier. As planes approached the speed of sound, they began to malfunction. In the film, Chuck Yeager figured out the controls would work once the plane hit the speed barrier, but only in reverse. It makes for a compelling movie—but it isn't true to life. Wright offers this illustration as an example of God's kingdom: it works the opposite way the world works. The empire tells us that powerful people are blessed. Religion tells us that pious people are blessed. The Beatitudes pronounce a different blessedness.

The Beatitudes should shock us, but we tend to domesticate them. We make them nice statements worthy of a needlepoint, some good advice from a wise teacher. But the Beatitudes are not just moral and ethical teachings; they are an announcement of the kingdom of God. They describe the new covenant God made with God's people in and through Jesus.

In addition to sugarcoating the fierceness of the Beatitudes, we tend to read them prescriptively, thinking the kingdom of God will come into being once we solve the world's problems.

For more than a decade, my church has participated in a program to provide food to hungry neighbors. Most people, including myself, initially participate in this program because we want to feel good about our service and ease our guilt about our abundance. We like to see people as projects for us to solve.

Every person who serves in the program regularly comes to realize a profound truth: brokenness is a human reality. They reflect on their own lives and their brokenness. We cease to see the other as a project to fix but just another broken person.

There is a saying in A.A.: all my best choices led me to this church basement, drinking mediocre coffee, admitting to another broken person that I am powerless to fix my own life. The simple beauty of A.A. is that we are all broken, and our solution comes from outside of us.

Blessed are those who don't have their stuff together. That is the best summary of the first few verses of the Beatitudes. The Beatitudes are a pronouncement of God's blessing. They are not a prescription to get God's blessing.

When we realize that blessing is something God has done and is already doing, it relieves us of our need to see people as a project to fix. In the Beatitudes, those who are blessed are those brave enough to trust God. Service is one mourner sitting with another mourner. Blessing is when one hungry person tells another hungry person where to find food. It is the conviction that Christ died for those who don't have their act together. And who among us does?

—*Everett Lees*

Thursday in the Fourth Week of Lent

What Do I Value?

Lay not up for yourselves treasures upon earth, where moth and rust doth corrupt, and where thieves break through and steal: but lay up for yourselves treasures in heaven, where neither moth nor rust doth corrupt and where thieves do not break through nor steal: for where your treasure is, there will your heart be also.

MATTHEW 6:19-21

One of my family's greatest treasures was my grandmother's cooking pot. There was nothing particularly special or unique about my grandmother's cooking pot. You could find them at any hardware store. But that cooking pot was a part of the fabric of my childhood.

Her cooking pot had dents and burnt places. The lid didn't quite fit as snugly as it should. The handles would burn you something fierce if you grabbed them with bare hands. There were scratches from where it had been scrubbed too much and too long. My grandmother had other cooking pots, newer ones, but this particular cooking pot knew its way around food.

On a good day, this pot was probably only worth about $20, but it was a treasure beyond measure. Love brewed and boiled in the cooking pot, stewed and steamed and shared. I can still remember the smell of my grandmother's soup filling the house, the taste of cinnamon and thyme, the slowly simmering pumpkin and sweet potatoes. My grandmother's soup was sunshine for the soul on wet, stormy days.

We often ate from that cooking pot at our kitchen table, which my grandmother's grandfather built. He was enslaved when he hand-carved the mahogany wood that became my makeshift desk when I did my homework. I played hide-and-seek around the table and even carved my name under it (don't let my mother know).

We lost both the table and the cooking pot almost 15 years ago. Somehow, in the renovation of our family home, the cooking pot was misplaced and probably discarded, and the table, looking rather beat up, was thought by the contractor to be useless. This was a massive loss to our family since we have so few family heirlooms. But the thing about these treasures was that they weren't so much about the objects themselves but what they symbolized.

I treasure these memories of deep love in my heart. I suspect this is what Jesus means when he tells us, "Where your treasure is, there will be your heart also."

Often, we too easily hold onto things as though they are the treasure. We desperately want to cling to things as though they are the conduits of God's love. But they never were—and never will be.

Our treasures are found in the places where love has been sown and grown. Our treasures are found in returning to another the love that was first given us. Our treasures are found in the places where we have encountered the holy.

As followers of Jesus who walk in the Way, we are reminded that we cannot bribe, beg, or buy our way to God. We cannot hold tight to treasures of things; instead, we are called to hitch our hearts to the treasure of love and abide there for a while.

—*Deon K. Johnson*

Friday in the Fourth Week of Lent

Love Never Fails

Charity suffereth long, and is kind; charity envieth not; charity vaunteth not itself, is not puffed up, doth not behave itself unseemly, seeketh not her own, is not easily provoked, thinketh no evil; Rejoiceth not in iniquity, but rejoiceth in the truth; Beareth all things, believeth all things, hopeth all things, endureth all things. Charity never faileth... And now abideth faith, hope, charity, these three ; but the greatest of these is charity.

1 Corinthians 13:4-8, 13

Be ye all of one mind, having compassion one of another, love as brethren, be pitiful, be courteous ... not rendering evil for evil, or railing for railing: but contrariwise blessing.

1 Peter 3:8-9a

"Love never fails" comes from a passage of scripture often used in weddings. The King James's translation offers "charity" as the word for this love. The Apostle Paul uses the word agape. Agape is one of the three Greek words for love used in the New Testament. There is eros, or "erotic love," and phileo, or "brotherly love." And there is agape, a "self-giving love," routinely shown to be the love God has for us. This agape love bears all things, believes all things, hopes all things, and endures all things. It is this self-giving love of God that never fails.

To set love in an extreme example, Paul writes that if he understands all mysteries and has faith so as to move mountains but has not love, he is nothing. If he were to give away everything he owns and hand over even his very life but has not love—has not a self-giving *agape* sense of being more concerned for the other person than oneself—then he is nothing.

The love within the Trinity is not merely a feeling or emotion. And so, God's love is not dependent on a spouse's likes and dislikes, job, mood, or anything else so changeable. God's love does not depend on a sibling's lovability. God's love does not depend on whether a friend lets you down. God's love for everyone else is a lot like God's love for you. This love is much more dependable than you or me on our best days.

This love that was in the very life of God before creation is the love that never fails. This is the love of Jesus, so that as he died on the cross, he could look out at those who killed him and say, "Father, forgive them, for they know not what they do."

In these words of forgiveness, God's love is more concerned about the other than the self. Jesus demonstrates how love is much more than a feeling. Agape love is a decision, an act of the will rather than an emotion. When we embrace agape love, we see others as God sees them—and act on this decision rather than out of our feelings of love.

Do you want to experience that sort of godly love for your friends, your family, or your spouse? Then, the love you have for them cannot start with you and go out to them. The love you have for others must begin with God. Ask God to give you this gift. Pray for God to reveal to you how God sees these other people, especially the difficult people in your life.

Love that is more concerned about others than yourself is not about self-loathing or being abused. Real love can also come with a hard edge, for it is not loving to become co-dependent or support someone in the abuse of their bodies with drugs—legal or illegal—or alcohol. Real love can mean setting clear boundaries. Love that is more concerned for the other can be lived in many ways that involve standing up to abuse and not letting it continue. But what agape can't do is to remain passive when someone is in need.

Use agape as the test for your actions. Trying to decide what to do? Put agape into the equation. Should you forgive? Should you pick up the phone and make a call? Should you write a letter? Should you make a visit? Setting aside people who have a pattern of abuse that you must avoid, in the many garden-variety painful relationships in your life, the answer is love. The decision to forgive or call or write or visit should not depend alone on whether you have been hurt or could be hurt. The answer should depend on answering the question, "How is God's love calling me to act? What person is this love calling me to be?"

—*Frank Logue*

Saturday in the Fourth Week of Lent

Living Together

Wherefore putting away lying, speak every man truth with his neighbor: for we are members one of another.... Let all bitterness, and wrath, and anger, and clamour, and evil speaking, be put away from you, with all malice: And be ye kind one to another, tenderhearted, forgiving one another, even as God for Christ's sake hath forgiven you.

EPHESIANS 4:25, 31-32

And above all these things put on charity, which is the bond of perfectness. And let the peace of Christ rule in your hearts.

COLOSSIANS 3:14-15

Put away lying, bitterness, wrath, anger, clamor, and evil speaking. Apparently, the Epistle writers have not seen the news lately. Today, if it weren't for such evil speech, we would have nothing at all to say. Many modern pundits say that our public discourse has reached an all-time low.

But think about it. The Epistles, like Ephesians and Colossians, were written at the height of the Roman Empire. At that time, Rome had a method of dealing with public discourse: often, they crucified anyone who did not toe the party line. Rome's public discourse was brutish and often violent.

The Epistle writers had no assumptions that all of Rome would somehow adopt their kindhearted methods of being in relationship with each other. No, these instructions were meant for the Church community as an alternative to the behavior of the day. At the time, the Church was quite small—maybe a hundred or two hundred people amid cities of thousands or hundreds of thousands. This Christian way of being in community was not a sideshow in the Roman world.

The early Church forged ahead anyway, offering a counter to the culture of the day. The Church was small, ignored by the culture, but its members discovered a God who loved all humanity and called us all to love one another. The Church kept repeating that message over and over again, even through times of persecution. Eventually, the culture listened, and Rome became Christian.

I think we have a lot in common with that early Church. We live in a time when the culture does not follow the ideas of community set forth in the Epistles. We live in a brutish and hateful time. And the Church is now small and ignored by the culture around it. But, like those early Christians, we have discovered a God who loves all humanity and asks us to love one another. Like those early Christians, we will strive to live by the precepts outlined in the Epistles that call us into beloved community. And we will keep on repeating the message of God's love, over and over, until it is heard.

—*Stephen Smith*

WORSHIPS

Fifth Week in Lent

A DISCIPLE WORSHIPS

Come away now from your workaday cares, your solitary communings. It is the Lord's own Day. Here is holy church—chapel or cathedral, it is all one—the solemn, happy place of God. Despite scorn and cynics and our shortcomings, we here are a sworn band. God's peace is upon us. All hell cannot part or affright us. Here is Presence—tremendous. God is our refuge and strength. He solves us from our sins. His mercy raises us up. Our voices join to adore and praise him for His glory. We hear his sure word: Christ the King ordering mankind's rescue. With the Body broken for us, he gives sacrament of his presence and makes us one body. We dedicate our offerings, for all things come of him, and of his own have we given him. Restored, reunited, recharged by his Spirit, we go out to victory with his blessing. It is God's worth, our worship.

AFFIRMATIONS: "I was glad when they said, we will go up to the House of the Lord." "I will pay Thee my vows in the midst of the Congregation." "The Church ... He hath purchased with His own blood." There is power in the aggregate the solitary cannot find.

For a disciple, worship is a good and necessary reminder of who we are not: God.

Our daily lives might tell us something different. We work and work and work. We often exert our control over things and people. We try to do things our way. We often end up placing ourselves in the center of our universe, lamenting that the whole thing would fall apart if we weren't there and/or in charge.

But when we worship, we let go of the mirage of control we think we possess. Worship reorients our world, reminding us that it is God—not us—who is the center of our universe and in charge. Worship gives us permission to de-center ourselves from the world and allows us to let go of the burden and weight that we carry from the illusion that we are in control.

Worship reminds us: we are the created, not the Creator.

In corporate worship, our eyes are opened to the diversity of thoughts, lives, and people around us. It reminds us that we truly are not alone on this journey of faith: that, yes, we may have differing opinions and come from different walks of life, but we are bound to one another through God's Spirit and God's love. Worship gives space to pause and express our interconnectedness as we share in the gifts of bread and wine together. It reminds us that the journey of faith is not a hero's or a champion's journey; it is a journey that we are on together, discerning how God is leading us to be God's incarnated presence in our neighborhoods.

Worship helps us discover the Zulu phrase *ubuntu*: I am because you are.

Worship gives us space to confess how doing things our way may not have worked. It gives us space to reflect on how doing things our way may have caused more harm than good. But it also reminds us that we are forgiven and opens the door for reconciliation.

Worship gives us insight into how small we are, specks of dust. And worship fills us with hope: this God is a God who is not just with us but for us as well. While we may be small, our God is mighty to save.

Through worship, we are not just reminded of who we are but whose we are. We belong to God.

And because we are God's, no matter what society or the world tries to say or determine who we are, the foundational truth is that we are God's beloved. Nothing we can say or do will make God love us less or more. God simply loves us because we are God's children.

—*Joseph Yoo*

Monday of the Fifth Week in Lent

Absolution from God's Altar

I saw also the Lord sitting upon a throne, high and lifted up, and his train filled the temple. Above it stood the seraphims: each one had six wings; with twain he covered his face, and with twain he covered his feet, and with twain he did fly. And one cried unto another, and said, Holy, holy, holy, is the Lord of hosts: the whole earth is full of his glory. And the posts of the door moved at the voice of him that cried, and the house was filled with smoke. Then said I, Woe is me! for I am undone; because I am a man of unclean lips, and I dwell in the midst of a people of unclean lips: for mine eyes have seen the King, the Lord of hosts. Then flew one of the seraphim unto me, having a live coal in his hand, which he had taken with the tongs from off the altar: And he laid it upon my mouth, and said, Lo, this hath touched thy lips: and thine iniquity is taken away, and thy sin purged.

Isaiah 6:1b-7

Yom Kippur, the Day of Atonement, is celebrated every year by faithful Jews. It is a time to seek God's forgiveness of sins and then pray for the strength to amend lives.

In the early days of the temple, prescribed liturgies offered instruction on proper observance. All the priests of the temple would gather in the morning and draw lots to see who would enter the temple into the Holy of Holies. Only once a year, on this day, could anyone enter the Holy of Holies. It was the resting place for the Ark of the Covenant and was thought to be the very seat of God's presence. In the Holy of Holies, the priest would sacrifice for his own sins and then offer sacrifice for the sins of the people. Afterward, the priest would come out of the temple and pronounce forgiveness on all and then offer a word from the Lord about the need for people to amend their lives.

Rabbinic literature offers one more instruction about the liturgies of that day. Before going into the temple, the priest who entered would have the other priests tie a rope around his ankle—just in case. After all, who knew what might happen upon entering this sacred place of God's very presence?

We have almost no record of a priest being pulled out. No doubt, almost every year, the same thing happened. The priest went in, performed the rituals, and came back out to give the message of God's love, forgiveness, and call for repentance.

We have no record of anything unusual happening until the year when the lot fell to Isaiah. Most years, the priest went in and came back out, and that was it. But Isaiah's year was different. This was the year that King Uzziah died. During Uzziah's 40-year reign, the kingdom had been stable and prosperous, and I suspect many people were worried about the future. Amid that anxiety, Isaiah goes into the Holy of Holies, and he sees the Lord! The temple shakes. The Seraphim, stone carvings of angels, become animated and fly around this inner sanctum. The temple fills with the smoke of the burnt offerings and incense.

The text does not say, but I am sure the priests outside were alarmed and began to pull on that rope. To his credit, Isaiah hung in there and got the message from God: the message of God's Holiness. Notice the message is about God's Holiness, not that of a human being. In a time of anxiety, the focus of God's people is not supposed to be on a human leader like Uzziah or even Isaiah but on God. God will lead us through times of anxiety. It is God whom we worship, not human leaders, no matter how great they are. And it is in acknowledging the Holiness of God that we have hope for the future, a future in the hands of God alone.

We may not have the temple anymore, but we do have the altar, the place where we proclaim the presence of God. Every time we partake in the eucharist, we follow the rituals and proclaim God's presence, love, forgiveness, and the call to amend our lives. It is nothing out of the ordinary. But it is in such ordinary things that our foundations shake, and God is revealed. And we are reminded, especially when times are bad, that our future lies in the hands of our most Holy God alone.

—*Stephen Smith*

Tuesday of the Fifth Week in Lent

Joyful Worship

O send out your light and your truth; let them lead me; let them bring me to your holy hill and to your dwelling.

Then I will go to the altar of God, to God my exceeding joy; and I will praise you with the harp, O God, my God.

Why are you cast down, O my soul, and why are you disquieted within me? Hope in God; for I shall again praise him, my help and my God.

PSALM 43:3-5

The first time I saw the inside of The Chapel of The Apostles at The School of Theology at Sewanee was not a happy occasion. I had come to Sewanee to discern whether I wanted to attend seminary there. Between all the information sessions and packed schedule, the "Come and See" weekend became a blur for me. We had walked past the chapel (affectionately dubbed "Cota") so many times that I knew it was there if I needed a place to pray. After a particularly intense conversation about financial aid, I sought refuge in the Lady Chapel. Kneeling in prayer before a statue of Our Lady, I poured out my tears and my heart to God in search of some answer.

After finishing my "ugly cry," I heard someone speaking inside the Church. I stopped breathing momentarily and listened as one of the senior seminarians practiced her sermon. She spoke so confidently of the love of God and so convincingly about God providing for us that the words blew my fears away. Much to her surprise, I emerged from the Lady Chapel and gave her a bit of a fright. She saw that I had been crying and apologized deeply for disturbing my prayers. I assured her it was no disturbance at all and that her sermon was an answer to my prayer.

Indeed, "Why are you cast down, O my soul, and why are you disquieted within me? Hope in God; for I shall again praise him, my help and my God."

Going to church has become pedestrian for some. We forget that we encounter the living and true God in our worship. We seek God in our prayers. We commune with God in our sacraments. We may even see the face of God in the faces of others.

Sometimes, circumstances darken our hearts and make us feel less than joyful. But God stands ready to hear those sorrows, absolve our sins, grant us healing, and even feed us with spiritual food. We who are called to the table can come for strength and solace. For renewal and pardon. We can come and encounter God, who longs for us to "taste and see that the Lord is good." And what joyful news this is!

As the psalmist writes, our desire to worship God should shine like the beam of a lighthouse in a storm, showing the way into the harbor. The psalmist writes in such a way that the reader can see the longing to worship, longing to be called to that holy place where thanks can be rendered to Almighty God. I worry that too often, we're occupied with whether we'll like the hymns or connect with the sermon to realize what a delight our worship can be.

But the psalmist asks us why our hearts are disquieted. Have we too easily forgotten who it is we've come to experience? God longs to be our exceeding joy, and with a God like ours who is "slow to chide and quick to bless," it's easy to see pathways to joy.

—*Tyler Richards*

Wednesday of the Fifth Week in Lent

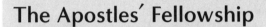

The Apostles' Fellowship

And they continued steadfastly in the apostles' doctrine and fellowship, and in breaking of bread, and in prayers.... And all that believed were together, and had all things common; And sold their possessions and goods, and parted them to all men, as every man had need. And they, continuing daily with one accord in the temple, and breaking bread from house to house, did eat their meat with gladness and singleness of heart.

ACTS 2:42, 44-46

I remember a Sunday years ago when this reading from Acts was part of the lectionary during the Easter season. A parishioner came out of the service and said, "I have never heard that reading before. I never knew the New Testament supported communism."

I was taken aback and did not know what to say. I cannot remember what I said in response, but I am sure I did not do the lesson justice. I invited the parishioner to come and talk with me, but he declined, saying, "I just thought it was funny."

Our culture has not been very kind to either communism or socialism. For most of the twentieth and twenty-first centuries, these political doctrines have been perceived as our enemies. So, it made me wonder how many people sitting in the pews might have been bothered by this quote from the Book of Acts. And it made me wonder what to say to the next person who asked me about the lesson.

So, what would I say?

First of all, I would emphasize that when these words were written, communism had not been invented. That doctrine would develop 1,700 years after the time of the Apostles.

Next, I would say that at this point in the history of the early Church, most Christians expected Jesus's imminent return and the end of the world. Why should possessions even matter when the world was about to end?

Then, I would say the kingdom of God that Jesus preached about is revealed in this lesson as a place where we share with others and no one is in need.

Then, I would talk about the kingdom of God because that's the crux of the story, even if it is not mentioned in the lesson itself. We could just as easily substitute the phrase "government of God." After all, kingdoms were a common form of government in the days of Jesus and the Apostles. And from Jesus's preaching and a lesson like this one from Acts, we have a blueprint for God's government. It is a place where all know the love of God, where all share, where none are in want or need, and where God is King.

This is where it gets difficult because movements across history have said they were dedicated to God as King, political leader, and sovereign of the nation. These movements are called theocracy or Christian nationalism. And throughout history, these movements have always brought out the worst in us Christians. The focus of a theocracy always seems to shift from care for one another to dominant power used to put down dissent with violence (consider the Puritans and how their early hopes morphed into the Salem Witch trials as just one example).

If we look at the words kingdom and God, maybe we should remember that God is the most important word. The kingdom or government is just a way to organize ourselves. If our focus is on God, then all will know the love of God, all will share, and none will be in want, just as the Book of Acts recounted about the early Church so many years ago.

—*Stephen Smith*

Thursday of the Fifth Week in Lent

Stand Within Her Gates

I was glad when they said unto me: Let us go into the house of the Lord. Our feet shall stand within thy gates: O Jerusalem.... Pray for the peace of Jerusalem: they shall prosper that love thee. Peace be within thy walls, and prosperity within thy palaces. For my brethren and companions' sakes, I will now say, Peace be within thee. Because of the house of the LORD our God I will seek thy good.

PSALM 122:1-2, 6-9

I've been fortunate to make the pilgrimage to Jerusalem, which I appreciate is a rare privilege. The labyrinthine streets of the old city are filled with the sensual experience of lives that have been lived out there for millennia that only the stones of the streets could recount. On my first day in Jerusalem, I got lost in the Old City and only managed to find my way out by accident—but what an adventure·it was to have done that.

Jerusalem is a city conceived, it seems, in worship. So much worship has happened in that city, along with much else. Jews, Muslims, and Christians all offer their prayers there, and so many journey there seeking God or a deeper knowledge of God.

Jerusalem is also an ideal. The scriptures continually point toward and pray for Jerusalem as a center of prayer, a house of prayer. But what if I told you there is a Jerusalem near you? What if I were to say there is such a place near to you that is bathed in prayer and engulfed in the presence of God? What if I also said that place is within and outside you and that you need both?

The Holy Spirit is not just a passive part of our lives but a living connection to God, the enlivening force of God tabernacled in our flesh. Our metaphorical heart is the place where the Holy Spirit abides with us and creates within us a dwelling for God. As such, we should take great care to show great care for our hearts, souls, and minds, cultivating within us a sense of the holy and making it a regular practice to clean out the cobwebs. Just as we show great respect for The Church of the Holy Sepulchre in Jerusalem, we should also respect the Ark that is our heart and think of what we put in there for God to live amongst.

Less metaphoric and more literal are the worship spaces where we gather. How bathed in prayer are those walls, altars, and kneelers? Visiting these spaces when our hearts are broken, when we desire to feel close to God, and when we want to know that we are truly praying on holy ground can be an amazing experience. Visiting those holy places and sitting where countless others have sat seeking the face of God connects us not only to God but also to the communion of saints in the places where those saints have gone before us, doing the same thing we are.

The challenge for us today is how to make our lives little "Jerusalems"—little centers of prayer, worship, and devotion to God. How can we draw others to stand within the gates of the holy by our words and actions?

—*Tyler Richards*

Friday of the Fifth Week in Lent

Pleasant Are Thy Courts

How amiable are thy dwellings: O Lord of hosts! My soul longeth, yea, even fainteth for the courts of the Lord: my heart and my flesh crieth out for the living God. Yea, the sparrow hath found an house, and the swallow a nest for herself, where she may lay her young, even thine altars, O Lord of hosts, my King, and my God. Blessed are they that dwell in thy house: they will be still praising thee…. They go from strength to strength, every one of them in Zion appeareth before God. Selah. O Lord God of hosts, hear my prayer: give ear, O God of Jacob. Behold, O God our shield, and look upon the face of thine anointed. For a day in thy courts is better than a thousand. I had rather be a doorkeeper in the house of my God, than to dwell in the tents of wickedness.

Psalm 84:1-3, 7-10

In 2011, I failed my ordination exams to become an elder in the United Methodist Church for the second time in a row. I felt like all the feelings I could feel were rolled up into one big ball of emotions.

Feelings of worthlessness and failure. How could I fail twice in a row? Feelings of anger and bitterness. How could they fail me twice in a row?

I was not in a good space emotionally, spiritually, and physically. And to be honest, I was also deeply embarrassed that I had failed two years in a row. Yet, I did not know how to express my lament, anger, embarrassment, and disappointment. I knew how I didn't want to spend my time: going to my dad's church for a revival.

Alas, I am a dutiful and obedient eldest Korean son, and I showed up to my dad's church—more out of obligation than for worship. The guest preacher was a dear friend to my parents and a talented musician. He has written many contemporary Christian songs in Korea and was here to preach and lead people in singing and praising. I was physically present, but my mind was elsewhere. Then, he started singing the one song of his that I knew.

I could never have anticipated how I would respond. For the first time that evening, my head was in the same space as my feet.

The music moved me—but so did the actual words. There's something poignant about hearing God's message in your mother tongue. Granted, my Korean has never been that good—most likely at kindergarten level, as that's when we left Korea. But hearing God's message in Korean always does something to me.

As the pastor led us in song, I sang along. And then all the angst, anger, bitterness, disappointment, and feelings of worthlessness started to wash away. I don't like public crying, but I couldn't help myself. While trying to hide my tears and stifle some unexpected sobs, I could not shake off this deep sense of being home—of being where God was.

Later in the service, we gathered around the centerpiece of many actual homes: the table. Despite aking the bread and wine with people were mostly strangers to me, I felt that I was home; that church was home. And not just this church but the Church—the holy spaces where we intentionally arrive to encounter God.

At this table, all of my angst, anger, and embarrassment washed away as I was re-membered into the body of Christ. Even though I had failed my ordination exams—twice—I was called upon to remember who I truly belonged to: not a denomination but God.

The joy of entering God's court comes from understanding that all we are and all we have are from God—that our lives belong to God and that we have a greater purpose.

When we truly allow ourselves to let go of ourselves and be in our Creator's presence, we will fully understand how a day in God's courts is better than a thousand elsewhere.

—*Joseph Yoo*

Saturday of the Fifth Week in Lent

Nunc Dimittis

And he came by the Spirit into the temple: and when the parents brought in the child Jesus, to do for him after the custom of the law, Then took he him up in his arms, and blessed God, and said, Lord, now lettest thou thy servant depart in peace, according to thy word: for mine eyes have seen thy salvation. Which thou hast prepared before the face of all people, A light to lighten the Gentiles, and the glory of thy people Israel.

LUKE 2:27-32

Where would I be without the faith of my grandmother? In many ways, she, like Mary and Joseph, brought me into the proverbial temple and entrusted me to the care of God with her prayers. She commended unto me that which she had received from someone else and, in doing so, demonstrated a deep faithfulness to her own trust in the gospel of Jesus Christ. I will forever credit my priesthood to her calling.

My children tear through the Church where I serve, barefoot and full of joy and giggles. My youngest has her spot at the rail where she stands patiently, hands folded in cherubic repose, waiting for me to come by and give her a blessing before I give my wife communion. My daughter gets upset if the service goes too long and shrieks when my wife won't let her rush to the altar rail whenever she wants. Whether driven there by a divine call or insistence that she go to the same spot every week, I cannot say. But I am confident that something within her responds to the holy, and the same is true for her older sister.

Our children look to us to see what faith looks like. They want to see what our family believes. While working on their own sense of self, they are also working on their sense of God and how we connect to God. Whether these experiences occur in the pews of the Baptist church that their grandmother attends or grand cathedral spaces that captivate their imaginations, they see it when we show them how to connect with God. What has been true in my own life is that my children notice and respect what I value as sacred as well. When I tell them something points us to God, they try that idea on for size, and very often, that holy moment lodges in their hearts and minds.

Mary and Joseph do for Jesus what was done for them and for those who came before them, a faith demonstrated by countless generations who continually whispered the words of the *Shema*, "Hear, O Israel: Adonai is our God, Adonai in One! Blessed is God's name; His glorious kingdom is forever and ever! And you shall love Adonai your God with all your heart, with all your soul, and with all your might."

The deacon with whom I serve, Mary Lynn Adams, told me about a conversation she had with my oldest daughter while

Emery was "helping" her set the table for a service one day. Mary Lynn was showing her the hosts in the ciborium and the various other accoutrements that sit on the altar. Mary Lynn even showed her the priest host that sits on the paten, waiting to be used during the consecration of the elements. Emery exclaimed, "Hey, that's the one that Daddy holds up and breaks before we take communion!"

"The bread that we break, is it not a sharing in the body of Christ? Because there is one bread, we who are many are one body, for we all partake of the one bread" (1 Corinthians 10:16b-17).

—*Tyler Richards*

SHARES

Holy Week

A DISCIPLE SHARES

That man upon his cross! What shall we do with him? Avert our look and pass by, and let a world lost haunt us forever? Or stand before him till we can stand no more, bowed to earth by His incredible love? It is not in death to move us so. It is God, willing for love and pity's sake to shear himself off into our hands and say, "Here, take my Life! Share Me!" It is not in death to remove him from us. He is with us now, the same offered life, the same love. No one loves the world like him. We tinker at it. He is saving it. Every wrong, every cry, every pang as the better struggles to be born, is at the instant in his heart.

What shall we do with him? He has only one offer: himself. He asks but one return: myself—but my real self. My prodigal rags of fear, pride, and sin… he strips them off and covers me with the best robe, his own. O, then I am changed. Now I live only to share my life, my powers, my mind, my money, my time, my newfound joy. Life changes from a taking game to a game of give-and-give-again.

RESOLUTION: Our Lord set his face like a flint to make this stage of the journey. Pray for strength to endure hardness like a good soldier of Jesus Christ. Sacrifice pettiness. Pray for grim purpose in the whole church.

My Cousin Vinny is a comedy about a New York lawyer who travels to Alabama to defend his cousin, who is falsely accused of murder. At the movie's end, the character, played by Marissa Tomei, an out-of-work hairdresser and mechanic, realizes the misidentification, leading to the murder charges being dismissed. The Buick Skylark driven by the defendant looks like a Pontiac Tempest the actual killers drove. She offers another option that matches the Tempest's mechanical specifications: a Corvette. As Tomei's character declares: "Nobody would confuse a Corvette with the Buick Skylark."

That is the scene we find on Palm Sunday. Pontius Pilate likely has traveled from his palace at Caesarea Philippi to Jerusalem for Passover. We can only imagine the pomp and circumstance as Pilate enters Jerusalem. The mighty Roman army lines the streets as Caesar's representative enters the city. To demonstrate their allegiance to Rome, dignitaries of the town welcome him with music and fanfare, celebrating his arrival. It must have been very impressive, as grand military parades often are.

Pilate and his army likely arrive on grand war horses as a reminder of Rome's power—a warning to any troublemakers in Jerusalem.

On the other side of the valley, Jesus and his disciples and followers travel to the city. Jesus instructs his disciples to go ahead of him, find a colt, and bring it to him to ride. Nobody would confuse a colt with a war horse.

Jesus enters as the Messianic hero, greeted with palm branches waving and people throwing their cloaks. We can imagine some people laughing at the juxtaposition of Pilate's entrance with Jesus's.

Jesus arrives for his enthronement not with an army but with a ragtag group of disciples and followers. Certainly, they think this is the week Jesus will take his throne and drive Rome out of the land. But Jesus's enthronement is not in a grand palace but outside the city walls. His crown is not lined with jewels but thorns that dig into his skin. The throne is not an impressive chair but a disgraceful tree.

Episcopal priest and author Fleming Rutledge calls the crucifixion a "godlessness" death. While crucifixion was not unusual in Jesus's day, it still bore the stigma and shame of death on a tree. Liberation theology scholar James Cone, reflecting on the cross and America's reliance on lynching for a similar purpose, writes, "The gospel of Jesus is not a rational concept to be explained in a theory of salvation, but a story about God's presence in Jesus's solidarity with the oppressed, which led to his death on the cross. What is redemptive is the faith that God snatches victory out of defeat, life out of death, and hope out of despair."

Christians are constantly tempted to want the war horse, but our king rides a donkey. We rather like the comforts our nation and economy provide, all the while cosplaying a prophet. We want the Corvette. We get the Buick Skylark.

—*Everett Lees*

Monday in Holy Week

The Imitation of Christ

We know that we have passed from death unto life, because we love the brethren. He that loveth not his brother abideth in death.... Hereby perceive we the love of God, because he laid down his life for us: and we ought to lay down our lives for the brethren. But whoso hath this world's good, and seeth his brother have need, and shutteth up his bowels of compassion from him, how dwelleth the love of God in him? My little children, let us not love in word, neither in tongue; but in deed and in truth.

1 JOHN 3:14, 16-18

Mature spiritual living shows up in the ways we imitate Christ. So many churches and religious institutions think the most important call for us is worshiping God. In truth, the most important and urgent thing is for us to imitate God. You can trace the pattern of Christian sin by tracking the times we have not imitated Jesus Christ. It is the gravest mistake the Church has made throughout the centuries: leaning more into worshiping Jesus Christ and demonstrating the Church's power rather than imitating Jesus Christ.

What does it mean to imitate Christ? An important early step is to actively deepen our faith by listening to the call of Jesus to follow me. Taking up the cross, living the Beatitudes, and praying for the grace to "preach the gospel at all times and when necessary, use words."

Imitating Jesus involves passing from death to life repeatedly. Called to die to self, we seek ways of serving and desiring the best for all we meet. Once again, we are called to accept that love is the foundation of all spiritual activity. We show that we are spiritually mature followers of Jesus by the way we love. Loving the world is a non-negotiable in imitating Christ; it is essential to the Christian way.

Imitating Christ is the most radical and important call we have been extended.

It is said that love self-manifests in and through actions. In the gospels and the Johannine epistles, the love of God made known in Jesus Christ manifests in and through Jesus's laying down his life. Jesus laid down his life because of his love for God and the world. He demonstrates the love of God by showing courage in the face of death. Jesus showed his love of God by laying down his life without anger, hate, shaming, or blaming others and by praying that those who crucified him be forgiven. This is how we are called to imitate Jesus Christ.

Jesus laid down his life for others, and we are to lay down our lives for others, too. There is no greater love, it is said, than to lay down one's life for a friend. Of course, we must remember that we believe Jesus laid down his life for the world. This invites us to lay down our lives for the world, too—especially those who are strangers to us and even our enemies. Imitating Jesus Christ is not for wimps.

Our passage for the day reminds us of the Parable of the Last Judgement in Matthew 25. Jesus taught explicitly and implicitly that we are called to imitate him by seeing in others the fullness of Jesus Christ. We imitate Jesus by living with an open heart of compassion: welcoming the stranger, the refugee, or the immigrant. Do we imitate Jesus Christ in our response to those at our borders? How do we imitate Jesus Christ in our response to those who are imprisoned?

Increasingly, we hear that Lent is not just a season in which we give something up. In Lent, we may also start new spiritual practices or revive holy activities we did in the past. How do we live out the love of Jesus Christ in both deed and truth? What does it mean for us to give our lives for others? How do we lay down our lives? These questions are intended to encourage us as we seek to respond to the invitation to imitate Jesus Christ.

Remember, imitating Jesus Christ is like loving and living marriage vows. We are committing to imitate Jesus Christ in good times and in bad, in sickness and health, for better or worse, until death.

—*Mark Francisco Bozzuti-Jones*

Tuesday in Holy Week

His Mind in Us

Look not every man on his own things, but every man also on the things of others. Let his mind be in you, which was also in Christ Jesus: Who, being in the form of God, thought it not robbery to be equal with God: but made himself of no reputation, and took upon him the form of a servant and was made in the likeness of men: and being found in fashion as a man, he humbled himself, and became obedient unto death, even the death of the cross.

PHILIPPIANS 2:4-8

As we make our way through Holy Week, we reflect on what it means that the disciple's life is one of sharing. Today, we turn to one of the earliest passages in the New Testament (you may have heard it read at services on Palm Sunday). It appears in Philippians, a letter Paul wrote to a church he deeply loved. It's a letter written from prison, though the call to rejoice reverberates throughout the letter. It's a letter written to disciples, and in this passage, Paul identifies an essential characteristic of disciples: that they have the mind of Christ. To illustrate what it means to have the mind of Christ, Paul quotes from a hymn already in existence, an early piece of liturgy that speaks about what it means to have the mind of Christ. It has a lot to do with sharing.

This hymn, which dates early in the history of the Jesus movement, speaks of Jesus who did not think it "robbery to be equal with God," as the King James Version puts it. Other, more recent translations say that equality with God is not something to be grasped or exploited. The mind of Christ is not about the me-first mentality that pervades our culture. It's not even necessarily about our rights. To have the mind of Christ is to avoid insistence on our virtue or what is owed to us. It's a posture of humility, which author C.S. Lewis describes this way: Humility is not thinking less of yourself; it's thinking of yourself less. That seems to be key to a life marked by sharing, in which we surrender our prerogatives for the good of another.

The hymn goes on to say that Jesus made himself of no reputation and took upon himself the form of servant made in the likeness of human beings. The mind of Christ is so oriented to sharing and focused on service to the other that it refuses to worry about reputation or what people are thinking. Truth be told, we cannot control what other people think of us. This perspective can set us free to be of service—and opportunities for service abound, always close at hand. My father-in-law, well into his 90s, will often call us first thing in the morning and ask: How can I help you today? Many people at that stage of life live with a list of ways family can attend to them. His commitment to service keeps him lively. To have the mind of Christ is to take on the role of a servant. In Mark's Gospel, Jesus says the Son of Man came to serve, not to be served. That kind of service is all about sharing and being generous with our time, energy, and other resources.

Finally, the ancient hymn says that Jesus humbled himself, obedient to the death, arguably one of the worst kinds of death imaginable. There is no limit to Jesus's willingness to share. To have the mind of Christ is to give without limit and to love unconditionally.

We may not be able to love in that unconditional manner, but we can move in that direction as we take steps to follow Jesus. As we walk through this Holy Week, may we, as disciples, grow in the ways we follow Jesus's example, living all of life in a spirit of sharing.

—*Jay Sidebotham*

Wednesday in Holy Week

In His Steps

Christ also suffered for us, leaving us an example, that ye should follow his steps: Who did no sin, neither was guile found in his mouth: Who, when he was reviled, reviled not again; when he suffered, he threatened not; but committed himself to him that judgeth righteously: Who his own self bare our sins in his own body on the tree, that we, being dead to sins, should live unto righteousness: by whose stripes ye were healed. For ye were as sheep going astray; but are now returned unto the Shepherd and Bishop of your souls.

1 PETER 2:21B-25

In the Holy Land, there is a church named St. Peter in Gallicantu. It was built over the supposed spot in the courtyard of Caiaphas, where Peter thrice betrayed Christ. The church has a large triptych icon that tells the story of Peter's arc of discipleship in three powerful images. The icons, made by Evgeni Kisets, show Peter's denial, Peter lamenting his sin, and the Risen Jesus calling Peter to mission.

A close investigation of the first icon shows Peter without his halo. The scene includes him talking to the woman who recognizes him as one of Jesus's followers, but Peter denies even knowing the man. In the middle of the icon, the pillar with the telltale rooster divides the two central characters, as the rooster heralds Jesus's prophecy about Peter's threefold betrayal. Jesus seems to gaze heartbreakingly into Peter's eyes, which no doubt sends him reeling into despair. Indeed, the second icon depicts that pain as Peter sits alone in a cave and weeps.

Interesting, however, is that Peter's halo is restored in this second icon. Here, in a cave that has become his own kind of tomb, a part of Peter is restored. This tomb cave was no accidental choice by the iconographer. It symbolizes that Peter is going through his own journey of death and resurrection by finally following true discipleship—which will always lead to the death of an old life of sin and being raised to new life with Christ.

You can't follow at a distance and be a disciple. In fact, there was even a blessing in the ancient world that stated: "May the dust of your rabbi be ever upon you." In other words, may you follow in your teacher's footsteps so closely that the dust they kick up falls on you. At this moment, Peter, though he is standing a far distance away from the crucifixion, may be closer to Christ than he has ever been before as he shares in a kind of death Jesus bore. His tomb is becoming his womb to true discipleship, for he is sharing with Jesus in this holy transformation and then will share that same transformation with the world.

Our scripture today comes from 1 Peter, a book in the New Testament that most scholars agree was not written by the disciple himself but instead attributed to him. Thus, we are invited to read this with the imagination of our hearts as though a much older Peter was now telling us what it means to share this holy ministry with Christ as his disciple. In the final icon, we see a post-resurrected Jesus talking with Peter at the same beach where they first met, and Jesus asks him to follow him as his disciple. There, he gives Peter the chance to profess his love of Jesus and his flock three times in a reversal of his previous denials and share in Jesus's ministry. What stands between them now is the shepherd's crook that Jesus entrusts to Peter as a symbol of his ministry going forward. I like to think of this epistle as giving us a glimpse into the heart of what this moment meant to Peter: "For to this you have been called, because Christ also suffered for you, leaving you an example, so that you should follow in his steps…For you were going astray like sheep, but now you have returned to the shepherd and guardian of your souls." This passage plainly shows us through the eyes of a now-wise disciple what it is to share in Jesus's life. Yes, we may sin. But we have also joined with Christ to follow him closely out of those old tombs of pain and despair. We do this not for ourselves but to follow Peter's mandate—to love and feed and share our whole selves with this world that is tended to by the shepherd and guardian of our souls.

May the dust of our Good Shepherd be ever upon us as we share in his mission to bring love and life to this world.

—*Hillary Raining*

Maundy Thursday

The Lord's Supper

And as they were eating, Jesus took bread, and blessed it, and brake it, and gave it to the disciples, and said, Take, eat; this is my body. And he took the cup, and gave thanks, and gave it to them, saying, Drink ye all of it; For this is my blood of the new testament, which is shed for many for the remission of sins. But I say unto you, I will not drink henceforth of this fruit of the vine, until that day when I drink it new with you in my Father's kingdom.

MATTHEW 26:26-29

Jesus gives us the gift of himself today in the institution of the Holy Eucharist. As he shares with his disciples, he asks us to share this sacred act with others in the hopes of living fully into his promise, uniting with him and all of creation in his Father's Kingdom.

Some of my most memorable occasions of eucharist were held in the most unusual of places. As a teenager, my high school youth group went on a retreat at the beach. There, by a fire and the ocean's waves, we celebrated the gift Jesus gave us. Later, as a new priest, I invited a community of parishioners, and we hiked up a mountain behind the church and gathered at the top of it on Ash Wednesday to share in the gifts of the bread and wine made holy.

But the most profound experience I ever had of sharing the communion of Christ's body and blood took place on a mission trip to Myanmar. A group of seminarians gathered, huddled together in a small hotel room. Bread and wine were not available for our service, so we ventured into the local community to find something that could be shared as the gifts of God for the people of God. One student landed upon a local staple, a type of coconut cake. Wine was nowhere to be found, so our leader used purified water instead. We had much to give thanks for on that day. Our journey was coming to an end, and we had witnessed the adverse effects of repressive violence and enforced poverty over the native Christian community. We needed Jesus that day, and we needed to offer thanks for our safety.

Our prayers began. We read the readings for the day and sang hymns. In the prayers of the people, we prayed for our friends back home, our new friends in Myanmar, and the thousands of people we met along our mission's journey. At the time of the Great Thanksgiving, our priest and mission leader gathered us in a circle. In each part of the prayers, she had one student pray out loud, accompanying her in the prayers. At the time when the words of institution were to be said, she asked for everyone to say the words of Jesus with her in a resounding commitment of solidarity and trust in the Living God. We sang a refrain of "Lord, prepare me to be a sanctuary" and quieted our hearts and minds to receive the body and blood of Christ with as much intentionality and hope as we could muster. Tears flowed, and a deep peace fell upon all gathered. Jesus was very much present in the form of eucharist that we had to offer that day. We were able to experience and see a glimpse of the kingdom of God.

Our life's journey with Christ invites us to look for Jesus in places we don't always expect. Our journey invites us to be surprised and, when we are, to give thanks to God. Such a gift was given to us on that day of the first eucharist, a gift of love, a gift of sustenance, a gift that continues to be shared with others, at every hour of every day, in virtually all parts of the world.

A few years ago, I wrote a hymn about our experience of the eucharist. The last verse was this:

> *Such a gift this is for us,*
> *Love so present and real*
> *Help spread your Word as life,*
> *Blessing hearts in this sacred meal.*

In Christ's sharing, it is time for us to truly give thanks. The eucharist is the ultimate gift that keeps on giving.

— *Troy Mendez*

Good Friday

The Three Hours

[No short reading suffices today, when of all days we should fast and confess our sins. Go to church. Hear the Story and accept His sacrifice. If duty detains you, meditate on the Passion. Repeat and think upon: "I live by faith in the Son of God, Who loved me and gave Himself for me."]

Good Friday is a day when words fail. Traditionally, Christians fast on this day to recognize Christ's suffering, but even this feels too small. On Good Friday, the best thing to do is acknowledge this insufficiency and attend to your parish's liturgical life. The liturgy manages to guide me through all the turbulent, complicated, unsettled feelings associated with this day.

Several years ago, my parish concluded the Good Friday liturgy by turning out all the lights except one spotlight on a large wooden cross while a soloist sang the hymn, "Were you there when they crucified my Lord?" On its face, this is an absurd question. We, living nearly two millennia after the crucifixion, were not there. As the song continues, it becomes clear that the writer wants us to imagine that we are there, at the foot of the cross, trembling, and to imagine further what our response might be to this terrifying, horrible sight.

A profound aspect of the traditional Jewish Passover Seder suggests that "in every generation, a person is obligated to see themselves as though they went out from Egypt." For Jews, the Passover is not just a historical event. It is a lived reality with social, ethical, and religious implications. The Passover is not something that happened to my distant ancestors. It is something that is happening to me and to us right now.

As Christians, we are not only called to be witnesses of the resurrection but also of the crucifixion. This means that we are called to understand and empathize with the suffering of Christ. Martin Luther King Jr., whose courageous witness for racial justice can best be seen as a sharing in the cruciform passion of Christ, said, "Christianity has always insisted that the cross we bear precedes the crown we wear. To be a Christian, one must take up his cross, with all its difficulties and agonizing and tension-packed content and carry it until that very cross leaves its mark upon us and redeems us to that more excellent way which comes only through suffering."

The crucifixion is not only something that happened in the distant past. It is happening. We are witnesses. This is true in a theological sense as well as an ethical one. Wherever human beings are subjected to death, violence, dehumanization, and terror, they are with Christ in his suffering. Where people are dishonored, disparaged, or persecuted for bearing witness to the Gospel of Jesus Christ in a world that grows increasingly hostile to its message of radical, challenging, inclusive love and forgiveness with no strings attached, this, too, is a sharing in Christ's suffering.

Often, when we experience or witness such suffering, our words fail, and so our bodies speak for us by trembling. We tremble now in terror, pain, and fear. But we are also witnesses of the resurrection, where our speechlessness is transformed into awe and wonder at a God who breaks through the darkness and continues to make all things new.

—*Marcus George Halley*

Holy Saturday

Resting in Hope

I have set the LORD always before me; because he is at my right hand, I shall not be moved. Therefore my heart is glad, and my glory rejoiceth: my flesh also shall rest in hope. For thou wilt not leave my soul in hell: neither wilt thou suffer thine Holy One to see corruption. Thou wilt shew me the path of life: in thy presence is fullness of joy; at thy right hand there are pleasures for evermore.

PSALM 16:8-11

They witnessed the imaginable. For three years, they had followed a rabbi like no other rabbi. He was different. He centered the outcast, the marginalized, the forgotten. He called tax collectors, fisher folk, and zealots to be his inner circle. For three years, they saw miracles, listened to parables, and discovered hope anew. Before their very eyes, they saw the blind receive their sight, the deaf regain their hearing, and even the dead brought back to life. This was the Messiah, the Anointed One of God.

Rabbi Jesus had to be the real deal, considering all the things that he did, said, and showed. Over 5,000 had gathered to hear him speak and were fed. Even the religious authorities were foiled by him. He was the one they had longed for. This ragtag band of misfit followers was a part of the rabbi's inner circle, and they knew he was special. They had planned on having front-row seats to the toppling of the oppressors as Jesus restored the people of God from subjugation and oppression.

But that was not to be. No army, no revolution, no uprising with this Messiah. Betrayal, denial, and dispersion were his legacy. He had been arrested, put on trial, and sentenced to die. They had watched as the crowds chanted, "Crucify! Crucify!" This was the moment they thought. Now, he would show them all that he was the one to wield the might of God. But then soldiers nailed Jesus to the cross. No fierce angels appeared with vengeance in their hands; there was no voice from the heavens, just all their hopes and dreams nailed to a shameful cross outside the city wall. They fled.

If this could happen to Jesus, the one they had pinned their hopes on, who had done so many miraculous things, what more would the Roman authorities do to them? Best to leave the city. Jesus was a failed messiah. He failed to live up to their expectations. He failed to show the might and power of God at the most crucial moment. What else could they do? They fled to the familiar place. They felt abandoned, alone, and even betrayed as Jesus hung there, breathing his last.

Their hearts were troubled as they left the city. They were afraid of what came next. The shared silence of the long walk was as heavy as their hearts. Night came as it always did. The sun rose in the morning, the birds sang just as brightly as they always had, and life went on as it always had. The shock of the last few days was finally sinking in as they gathered behind fear-locked doors. They were adrift and bereft. They entered the place of unknowing.

We are all familiar with the place of unknowing we call Holy Saturday. We have all heard the devastating news; we have walked the long path of the heavy-hearted. Like the disciples, we have wondered where God was hiding when we needed God the most. We have each experienced the betrayal and anger that inhabited the disciples of Jesus.

But even in that place of unknowing, the in-between places of our lives, God is there. God's presence fills the place of unknowing, especially when our hearts are too broken to perceive it. God has carried the anguish and pain of a heart broken time and time again. And as Jesus promised the disciples then and promises us now, God never leaves or forsakes us.

The sun will shine, the birds will chirp, and the world will tick on along its designated pathways, much as we would turn back time. Our hope, which breaks into every aspect of the place of unknowing, of the in-between place, of the Holy Saturdays of our lives, comes with the dawning of a new day.

Early in the morning, while it was still dark…

—*Deon K. Johnson*

Easter Day

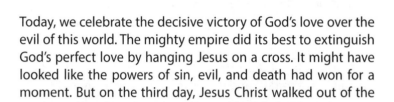

Today, we celebrate the decisive victory of God's love over the evil of this world. The mighty empire did its best to extinguish God's perfect love by hanging Jesus on a cross. It might have looked like the powers of sin, evil, and death had won for a moment. But on the third day, Jesus Christ walked out of the tomb, and in that moment, we could all behold God's grace and mercy triumphant. Yes, God's grace and mercy will always have the last word.

On Easter, we rally under the banner of the Lamb of God. Jesus Christ is risen from the dead, and he reigns this very day from his throne in heaven at his Father's right hand. Jesus loves you, and he is your advocate. Jesus loves you, and he wants you to know the transforming power of his grace and mercy.

Sin, evil, and death are, of course, real. Tyrants run amok. Division grows. Fear abounds. In the church, it is no different. Some leaders say that we must make peace with decline, and we will never have enough to fund the mission that Jesus Christ has given us. But we must not accept the claim that death, evil, and sin are sovereign. They do not define reality. Our reality is shaped by the love of God, which has been present in our universe from the moment of creation and will manifest fully at the end of time. Today, our task is to keep our eyes on that deep truth, which is more real than fleeting illusions of fear and sin.

How do we do it? How can we keep ourselves oriented toward Jesus Christ, who has suffered, died, risen, and ascended into heaven for us? We keep ourselves rooted with daily prayer, regular scripture study, faithful worship attendance, and all the other ancient and time-tested ways of a disciple. This Easter is the perfect time to commit or recommit to the disciple's way.

Let us go forth! Let us go forth in our onward journey, moving forward in a life of transformed faith. Let us go forth as a church, bearing Christ's grace and mercy into the whole world.

—*Scott Gunn*

A DISCIPLE CONTINUES

The enemy expects us to slacken now. Our God beckons us on. He promises: "If ye continue in my word, then are ye truly my disciples." We have our hand to the plow. Let's not turn back. Get a new grip on your discipleship. Keep up the rhythm of: "turn, follow, learn, pray, serve, worship, and share." Don't fail the Lord. Don't let the church down. The enemy expects to say of us: "You see, they don't mean business. They are petty. They have no pluck. They want their kingdom for themselves. They don't intend to change the world." Give that the lie! Join the Forward Movement for duration. Make it a real push forward of the kingdom. There are great books that give light. Ask your Rector. Stir for a program of new life for all.

O Lord Jesus Christ, who hast taught us always to pray and not to faint, we lift up to thy mercy the need of thy Church. And since thou hast given us the resolve to go forward and not back, grant to the leaders of our Forward Movement to be both wise and daring disciples, and to thy people a heart to follow them, for thy sake who art with the Father and the Holy Spirit one God world without end. Amen.

We pray thee, O God, for thy blessing upon the Forward Movement of thy Church. Use it, we beseech thee, to open our eyes to the needs of all for the Gospel of Christ, and to the opportunities that lie before the Church to extend his kingdom. Stir up, O Lord, the wills of all thy people to share in this work of gladness of heart and self-sacrificing spirit; and let not our purpose slack until the kingdoms of this world have become the kingdom of our God and of his Christ. Amen.

About the Authors

Mark Francisco Bozzuti-Jones is an Episcopal priest at Trinity Church Wall Street in New York City. He serves as the priest and director for spiritual formation at Trinity Retreat Center in West Cornwall, Connecticut. Born in Jamaica and fluent in Portuguese, Mark has a wide range of experience, including 14 years of Jesuit training and work as a missionary in Belize, Brazil, and Guyana. He is an award-winning author; recent books include *God Created, Jesus the Word, The Gospel of Barack Hussein Obama According to Mark, The Rastafari Book of Common Prayer, Absalom Jones: America's First Black Priest,* and *Face to the Rising Sun: Reflections on Spirituals and Justice.*

Chris Corbin is the rector of Trinity Episcopal Church in Oshkosh, Wisconsin, where he lives with his wife, who is also a priest, their two daughters, and three cats. He is editor-in-chief of *Earth & Altar*, a publication that promotes conversations around inclusive orthodoxy. Outside of church-related activities, Chris also enjoys graphic design, gardening, and traditional woodworking.

Scott Gunn is the executive director of Forward Movement. He travels widely as a preacher, speaker, and retreat leader. On Sundays, when he is not traveling, he serves as a priest associate at Christ Church in Glendale, Ohio. He is the author of several books; his most recent book is *Easter Triumph, Easter Joy: Meditations for the Fifty Days of Eastertide*. Before serving at Forward Movement, Scott was a parish priest in the Diocese of Rhode Island. Before that, he had a career in information technology. Scott was educated at Yale Divinity School, Brown University, and Luther College. He lives in Cincinnati with his spouse, Sherilyn Pearce, who is also an Episcopal priest.

Marcus George Halley is college chaplain and dean of spiritual and religious life at Trinity College, Hartford, Connecticut. Prior to serving Trinity College, Marcus served parishes and dioceses in West Missouri, Minneapolis, and Connecticut. He holds degrees from Johnson C. Smith University, Interdenominational Theological Center, and the School of Theology at the University of the South, with his most recent degree, doctor of ministry, focusing on liturgy and mission in the New Apostolic Age. He publishes a weekly Substack newsletter called "Everyday Liturgist." He and his husband—Curtis Farr, an Episcopal priest—live in Fairfield, Connecticut.

Deon K. Johnson serves as the bishop of the Diocese of Missouri. He is the first black, first gay, and first immigrant elected as bishop of this diocese. Johnson was born and raised in a small village on the Caribbean island of Barbados and immigrated to New York at the age of 14. His passion for social justice and racial reconciliation has shaped his ministry as bishop. Deon's service to the wider church community includes the Executive Council of the Episcopal Church, the Taskforce for Liturgical and Prayer Book Revision, and the Office of African Descent Ministries.

Everett Lees is the vicar of Christ Church in Tulsa, Oklahoma. He enjoys annoying his wife and running his three kids to activities when he is not helping the local police solve murders. He is a 6w5, Hufflepuff who excels at being an introvert.

Frank Logue serves as the bishop of the Episcopal Diocese of Georgia. He previously served as the canon to the ordinary for the same diocese. He has been active in church governance, including as a member of the Executive Council of the Episcopal Church.

His first call was as the church planter for King of Peace Episcopal Church in Kingsland, Georgia.

Troy Mendez lives in Phoenix, Arizona, and serves as executive director of the Episcopal Evangelism Society. Previously, Troy served as dean of Trinity Episcopal Cathedral, a historic and vibrant downtown Phoenix congregation. He is active on the boards of Virginia Theological Seminary and The General Theological Seminary of the Episcopal Church. He is passionate about the church offering to all people a sense of belonging and the grace of new life given to us in Jesus Christ.

Hugo Olaiz is the associate editor for Latino/Hispanic resources at Forward Movement. He lives in Oxford, Ohio, with his husband, their son, and two dogs.

Anna Olson is a graduate of Union Theological Seminary and Stanford University. She currently serves as director of the School for Christian Faith and Leadership in the Episcopal Diocese of Washington. Ordained in 2000, Anna has served six multicultural and multilingual congregations in the dioceses of Washington and Los Angeles and has done development and interfaith organizing work in human rights and economic justice. She is the author of *Claiming Resurrection in the Dying Church: Freedom Beyond Survival* and has published a number of articles.

Hillary Raining serves as the rector of St. Christopher's Episcopal Church in Gladwyne, Pennsylvania. She is also an author, seminary teacher, spiritual director, yoga and meditation instructor, beekeeper, and forest therapist. She is the proud founder of The Hive (thehiveapiary.com), an online spirituality and wellness community that helps bring ancient spiritual practices to modern-day mystics. You can find out more about Hillary at hillaryraining.com.

Tyler Richards is an Episcopal priest serving at St. Anne's Episcopal Church in De Pere, Wisconsin. He is also an avid birder, vocalist, and gardener. He enjoys spending free time with his wife and his beautiful daughters, usually somewhere in Michigan's Upper Peninsula. Tyler is also discerning a vocation with The Order of Christ our Saviour.

Richard H. Schmidt was editor and director of Forward Movement from 2005 to 2012. He previously served parishes in West Virginia, Missouri, Pennsylvania, and Alabama. He has written seven books on Christian spirituality. Now retired, he and his wife Pam live in Louisville, Kentucky.

Stephen Smith, an Episcopal priest, spent 37 years in parish ministry, serving in small towns, an industrial town, and a large suburban congregation. He has served the Episcopal Preaching Foundation in many capacities for more than 15 years, including teaching and preaching at conferences, chairing the Preaching Excellence Program (PEP), and developing the Lay Preacher Training program. His publications include *Saving Salvation: The Amazing Evolution of Grace* and numerous articles and sermons for Forward Movement and others. Though his triathlon days are over, Stephen remains an avid exercise enthusiast. In addition, a couple of weekends each month, he plays guitar in a classic rock band for fun. The name of the band? Revdup.

Jay Sidebotham lives in Wilmington, North Carolina, where he serves as a consultant with RenewalWorks, a ministry of Forward Movement, and is pursuing his vocation as a visual artist. Ordained to the priesthood in 1991, Jay served parishes in Rhode Island, Washington, D.C., North Carolina, New York, and Illinois. He attended Union Seminary in New York. Prior to that course of study, he worked in illustration, graphic design, and advertising in Manhattan. He also worked as an animator for *Schoolhouse Rock*. He considers it a great privilege to create cartoons for the Episcopal Church (there's a lot of material.) He is married to Frances Murchison. They have two adult children, each married, and four quite splendid grandchildren.

Kate E. Wesch is a follower of Jesus, a spouse, mother, friend, avid hiker, and colleague. She serves as the parochial vicar at Epiphany, Seattle. She has served full-time in parish ministry since 2007 and is passionate about the church's capacity to transform those whom God calls to our spaces. She has particular interest in inspiring Episcopalians to read and study the Bible in community as a means of inspiring discipleship.

Joseph Yoo is the vicar of Mosaic Episcopal Church in Pearland, Texas, a suburb of Houston. He lives in Houston with his wife, Rahel, son, Nathanael, and their tortoise, Dae Dae, who just may outlive them all. He is the author of *When the Saints Go Flying In*.

***The Editor*: Richelle Thompson** has edited more than 100 books for Foward Movement and is also the editor of *Forward Day by Day*. In addition, she runs a writing, editing, and project management consulting company, Crown Communications. She and her husband, the Rev. Jeffrey Queen, have two adult children and two grandchildren, and they live and serve in Northern Kentucky.

DAILY READINGS:
New Revised Standard Version

Ash Wednesday

You Need Me

Listen! I am standing at the door, knocking; if you hear my voice and open the door, I will come in to you and eat with you, and you with me.

REVELATION 3:20

And as he sat at dinner in the house, many tax collectors and sinners came and were sitting with him and his disciples. When the Pharisees saw this, they said to his disciples, "Why does your teacher eat with tax collectors and sinners?" But when he heard this, he said, "Those who are well have no need of a physician, but those who are sick.... For I have come to call not the righteous but sinners."

MATTHEW 9:10-12, 13B

Thursday

How Much Do You Care?

Listen! A sower went out to sow. And as he sowed, some seeds fell on the path, and the birds came and ate them up. Other seeds fell on rocky ground, where they did not have much soil, and they sprang up quickly, since they had no depth of soil. But when the sun rose, they were scorched; and since they had no root, they withered away. Other seeds fell among thorns, and the thorns grew up and choked them. Other seeds fell on good soil and brought forth grain, some a hundredfold, some sixty, some thirty. Let anyone with ears listen!

MATTHEW 13:3B-9

Friday

Simple? Troubled? Welcome.

At that time Jesus said, "I thank you, Father, Lord of heaven and earth, because you have hidden these things from the wise and the intelligent and have revealed them to infants; yes, Father, for such was your gracious will. All things have been handed over to me by my Father; and no one knows the Son except the Father, and no one knows the Father except the Son and anyone to whom the Son chooses to reveal him. "Come to me, all you that are weary and are carrying heavy burdens, and I will give you rest. Take my yoke upon you, and learn from me; for I am gentle and humble in heart, and you will find rest for your souls. For my yoke is easy, and my burden is light."

MATTHEW 11:25-30

Saturday

The World´s Hope

Then turning to the disciples, Jesus said to them privately, "Blessed are the eyes that see what you see! For I tell you that many prophets and kings desired to see what you see, but did not see it, and to hear what you hear, but did not hear it."

LUKE 10:23-24

Jesus said to her, "Everyone who drinks of this water will be thirsty again, but those who drink of the water that I will give them will never be thirsty. The water that I will give will become in them a spring of water gushing up to eternal life."

JOHN 4:13-14

First Week in Lent
A Disciple FOLLOWS

Monday

Here is Certainty

When John heard in prison what the Messiah was doing, he sent word by his disciples and said to him, "Are you the one who is to come, or are we to wait for another?" Jesus answered them, "Go and tell John what you hear and see: the blind receive their sight, the lame walk, the lepers are cleansed, the deaf hear, the dead are raised, and the poor have good news brought to them. And blessed is anyone who takes no offense at me."

MATTHEW 11:2-6

Tuesday

Meant For Us All

In the morning, while it was still very dark, he got up and went out to a deserted place, and there he prayed. And Simon and his companions hunted for him. When they found him, they said to him, "Everyone is searching for you." He answered, "Let us go on to the neighboring towns, so that I may proclaim the message there also; for that is what I came out to do."

MARK 1:35-38

Wednesday

Quibbles Can't Stop Him

Again he entered the synagogue, and a man was there who had a withered hand. They watched him to see whether he would cure him on the sabbath, so that they might accuse him. And he said to the man who had the withered hand, "Come forward." Then he said to them, "Is it lawful to do good or to do harm on the sabbath, to save life or to kill?" But they were silent. He looked around at them with anger; he was grieved at their hardness of heart and said to the man, "Stretch out your hand." He stretched it out, and his hand was restored.

MARK 3:1-5

Thursday

Right At Any Cost

Then they came to Jerusalem. And he entered the temple and began to drive out those who were selling and those who were buying in the temple, and he overturned the tables of the money changers and the seats of those who sold doves; and he would not allow anyone to carry anything through the temple. He was teaching and saying, "Is it not written,

> *'My house shall be called a house of prayer for all the nations'? But you have made it a den of robbers."*

And when the chief priests and the scribes heard it, they kept looking for a way to kill him.

MARK 11:15-18A

Friday

Servant of All

He got up from the table, took off his outer robe, and tied a towel around himself. Then he poured water into a basin and began to wash the disciples' feet and to wipe them with the towel that was tied around him. After he had washed their feet, had put on his robe, and had returned to the table, he said to them, "Do you know what I have done to you? You call me Teacher and Lord—and you are right, for that is what I am. So if I, your Lord and Teacher, have washed your feet, you also ought to wash one another's feet. For I have set you an example, that you also should do as I have done to you.

JOHN 13:4-5, 12-15

Saturday

The Price He Paid

Two others also, who were criminals, were led away to be put to death with him. When they came to the place that is called The Skull, they crucified Jesus there with the criminals, one on his right and one on his left. Then Jesus said, "Father, forgive them; for they do not know what they are doing." And they cast lots to divide his clothing. And the people stood by, watching; but the leaders scoffed at him, saying, "He saved others; let him save himself if he is the Messiah of God, his chosen one!"

LUKE 23:32-35

Second Week in Lent
A Disciple LEARNS

Monday

Jesus's Secret

*Meanwhile the disciples were urging him, "Rabbi, eat something."
But he said to them, "I have food to eat that you do not know about."
So the disciples said to one another, "Surely no one has brought him
something to eat?" Jesus said to them, "My food is to do the will of
him who sent me and to complete his work.*

JOHN 4:31-34

Tuesday

The Kingdom First

*And do not keep striving for what you are to eat and what you are
to drink, and do not keep worrying. For it is the nations of the world
that strive after all these things, and your Father knows that you need
them. Instead, strive for his kingdom, and these things will be given
to you as well. For where your treasure is, there your heart will be also.*

LUKE 12:29-31, 34

Wednesday

Don't Be a Fool

The land of a rich man produced abundantly. And he thought to himself, "What should I do, for I have no place to store my crops?" Then he said, "I will do this: I will pull down my barns and build larger ones, and there I will store all my grain and my goods. And I will say to my soul, 'Soul, you have ample goods laid up for many years; relax, eat, drink, be merry.' But God said to him, 'You fool! This very night your life is being demanded of you. And the things you have prepared, whose will they be?" So it is with those who store up treasures for themselves but are not rich toward God.

LUKE 12:16B-21

Thursday

God and My Neighbor

One of the scribes came near and heard them disputing with one another, and seeing that he answered them well, he asked him, "Which commandment is the first of all?" Jesus answered, "The first is, 'Hear, O Israel: the Lord our God, the Lord is one; you shall love the Lord your God with all your heart, and with all your soul, and with all your mind, and with all your strength.' The second is this, 'You shall love your neighbor as yourself.' There is no other commandment greater than these."

MARK 12:28-31

Friday

Related by Will

Then his mother and his brothers came; and standing outside, they sent to him and called him. A crowd was sitting around him; and they said to him, "Your mother and your brothers and sisters are outside, asking for you." And he replied, "Who are my mother and my brothers?" And looking at those who sat around him, he said, "Here are my mother and my brothers! Whoever does the will of God is my brother and sister and mother."

MARK 3:31-35

Saturday

You Do It to Him

"For I was hungry and you gave me food, I was thirsty and you gave me something to drink, I was a stranger and you welcomed me, I was naked and you gave me clothing, I was sick and you took care of me, I was in prison and you visited me." Then the righteous will answer him, "Lord, when was it that we saw you hungry and gave you food, or thirsty and gave you something to drink? And when was it that we saw you a stranger and welcomed you, or naked and gave you clothing? And when was it that we saw you sick or in prison and visited you?" And the king will answer them, "Truly I tell you, just as you did it to one of the least of these who are members of my family, you did it to me."

MATTHEW 25:35-40

Third Week in Lent
A Disciple PRAYS

Monday

The Lord's Prayer

He was praying in a certain place, and after he had finished, one of his disciples said to him, "Lord, teach us to pray, as John taught his disciples." He said to them, "When you pray, say: Father, hallowed be your name. Your kingdom come. Give us each day our daily bread. And forgive us our sins, for we ourselves forgive everyone indebted to us. And do not bring us to the time of trial."

LUKE 11:1-4

Tuesday

Tell Your Father

So I say to you, Ask, and it will be given you; search, and you will find; knock, and the door will be opened for you. For everyone who asks receives, and everyone who searches finds, and for everyone who knocks, the door will be opened. Is there anyone among you who, if your child asks for a fish, will give a snake instead of a fish? If you then, who are evil, know how to give good gifts to your children, how much more will the heavenly Father give the Holy Spirit to those who ask him!

LUKE 11:9-11,13

Wednesday

Turn Worry to Thanks

Do not worry about anything, but in everything by prayer and supplication with thanksgiving let your requests be made known to God. And the peace of God, which surpasses all understanding, will guard your hearts and your minds in Christ Jesus. Finally, beloved, whatever is true, whatever is honorable, whatever is just, whatever is pure, whatever is pleasing, whatever is commendable, if there is any excellence and if there is anything worthy of praise, think about these things.

PHILIPPIANS 4:6-8

Thursday

Prayer in Crisis

And going a little farther, he threw himself on the ground and prayed that, if it were possible, the hour might pass from him. He said, "Abba, Father, for you all things are possible; remove this cup from me; yet, not what I want, but what you want." He came and found them sleeping; and he said to Peter, "Simon, are you asleep? Could you not keep awake one hour? Keep awake and pray that you may not come into the time of trial; the spirit indeed is willing, but the flesh is weak."

MARK 14:35-38

Friday

Make Prayer Real

And whenever you pray, do not be like the hypocrites; for they love to stand and pray in the synagogues and at the street corners, so that they may be seen by others. Truly I tell you, they have received their reward. But whenever you pray, go into your room and shut the door and pray to your Father who is in secret; and your Father who sees in secret will reward you.

MATTHEW 6:5-6

Saturday

God Prays in Us

Likewise the Spirit helps us in our weakness; for we do not know how to pray as we ought, but that very Spirit intercedes with sighs too deep for words. And God, who searches the heart, knows what is the mind of the Spirit, because the Spirit intercedes for the saints according to the will of God. We know that all things work together for good for those who love God.

ROMANS 8:26-28A

Fourth Week in Lent
A Disciple SERVES

Monday

You Serve Christ

And whatever you do, in word or deed, do everything in the name of the Lord Jesus, giving thanks to God the Father through him. Whatever your task, put yourselves into it, as done for the Lord and not for your masters…you serve the Lord Christ.

COLOSSIANS 3:17, 23, 24B

Whoever wishes to be great among you must be your servant, and whoever wishes to be first among you must be your slave; just as the Son of Man came not to be served but to serve, and to give his life a ransom for many.

MATTHEW 20:26B-28

Tuesday

And So Serve Others

Owe no one anything, except to love one another; for the one who loves another has fulfilled the law. Love does no wrong to a neighbor; therefore, love is the fulfilling of the law.

ROMANS 13:8,10

Bear one another's burdens, and in this way you will fulfill the law of Christ.

GALATIANS 6:2

We who are strong ought to put up with the failings of the weak, and not to please ourselves.

ROMANS 15:1

Wednesday

The Beatitudes

"Blessed are the poor in spirit, for theirs is the kingdom of heaven. "Blessed are those who mourn, for they will be comforted. "Blessed are the meek, for they will inherit the earth. "Blessed are those who hunger and thirst for righteousness, for they will be filled. "Blessed are the merciful, for they will receive mercy. "Blessed are the pure in heart, for they will see God. "Blessed are the peacemakers, for they will be called children of God.

MATTHEW 5:3-9

Thursday

What Do I Value?

Do not store up for yourselves treasures on earth, where moth and rust consume and where thieves break in and steal; but store up for yourselves treasures in heaven, where neither moth nor rust consumes and where thieves do not break in and steal. For where your treasure is, there your heart will be also.

MATTHEW 6:19-21

Friday

Love Never Fails

Love is patient; love is kind; love is not envious or boastful or arrogant or rude. It does not insist on its own way; it is not irritable or resentful; it does not rejoice in wrongdoing, but rejoices in the truth. It bears all things, believes all things, hopes all things, endures all things.

Love never ends. But as for prophecies, they will come to an end; as for tongues, they will cease; as for knowledge, it will come to an end....And now faith, hope, and love abide, these three; and the greatest of these is love.

1 CORINTHIANS 13:4-8, 13

Finally, all of you, have unity of spirit, sympathy, love for one another, a tender heart, and a humble mind. Do not repay evil for evil or abuse for abuse; but, on the contrary, repay with a blessing.

1 PETER 3:8-9A

Saturday

Living Together

So then, putting away falsehood, let all of us speak the truth to our neighbors, for we are members of one another. Put away from you all bitterness and wrath and anger and wrangling and slander, together with all malice, and be kind to one another, tenderhearted, forgiving one another, as God in Christ has forgiven you.

EPHESIANS 4:25, 31-32

Above all, clothe yourselves with love, which binds everything together in perfect harmony. And let the peace of Christ rule in your hearts, to which indeed you were called in the one body. And be thankful.

COLOSSIANS 3:14-15

Fifth Week in Lent
A Disciple WORSHIPS

Monday

Absolution from God's Altar

I saw the Lord sitting on a throne, high and lofty; and the hem of his robe filled the temple. Seraphs were in attendance above him; each had six wings: with two they covered their faces, and with two they covered their feet, and with two they flew. And one called to another and said: "Holy, holy, holy is the LORD of hosts; the whole earth is full of his glory." The pivots on the thresholds shook at the voices of those who called, and the house filled with smoke.

And I said: "Woe is me! I am lost, for I am a man of unclean lips, and I live among a people of unclean lips; yet my eyes have seen the King, the LORD of hosts!" Then one of the seraphs flew to me, holding a live coal that had been taken from the altar with a pair of tongs. The seraph touched my mouth with it and said: "Now that this has touched your lips, your guilt has departed and your sin is blotted out."

ISAIAH 6:1A-7

Tuesday

Joyful Worship

O send out thy light and thy truth, that they may lead me: and bring me unto thy holy hill, and to thy tabernacles. Then will I go unto the altar of God, unto God my exceeding joy: yea, upon the harp will I praise thee, O God my God. Why art thou cast down, O my soul? and why art thou disquieted within me? hope in God: for I shall yet praise him, who is the health of my countenance, and my God.

PSALM 43:3-5

Wednesday

The Apostles' Fellowship

They devoted themselves to the apostles' teaching and fellowship, to the breaking of bread and the prayers. All who believed were together and had all things in common; they would sell their possessions and goods and distribute the proceeds to all, as any had need. Day by day, as they spent much time together in the temple, they broke bread at home and ate their food with glad and generous hearts.

ACTS 2:42, 44-46

Thursday

Stand Within Her Gates

I was glad when they said to me, "Let us go to the house of the LORD!"
Our feet are standing within your gates, O Jerusalem.
Pray for the peace of Jerusalem: "May they prosper who love you.
Peace be within your walls, and security within your towers."
For the sake of my relatives and friends I will say,
*   "Peace be within you."*
For the sake of the house of the LORD our God, I will seek your good.

PSALM 122:1-2, 6-9

Friday

Pleasant Are Thy Courts

How lovely is your dwelling place, O LORD of hosts!
My soul longs, indeed it faints for the courts of the LORD;
my heart and my flesh sing for joy to the living God.
Even the sparrow finds a home, and the swallow a nest for herself,
where she may lay her young, at your altars, O LORD of hosts,
my King and my God.
They go from strength to strength; the God of gods will be seen
in Zion.
O LORD God of hosts, hear my prayer; give ear, O God of Jacob! Selah
Behold our shield, O God; look on the face of your anointed.
For a day in your courts is better than a thousand elsewhere. I would
rather be a doorkeeper in the house of my God than live in the
tents of wickedness.

PSALM 84:1-3, 7-10

Saturday

Nunc Dimittis

Guided by the Spirit, Simeon came into the temple; and when the
parents brought in the child Jesus, to do for him what was customary
under the law, Simeon took him in his arms and praised God, saying,
"Master, now you are dismissing your servant in peace, according
to your word; for my eyes have seen your salvation, which you have
prepared in the presence of all peoples, a light for revelation to the
Gentiles and for glory to your people Israel."

LUKE 2:27-32

Holy Week
A Disciple SHARES

Sunday

Monday

The Imitation of Christ

We know that we have passed from death to life because we love one another. Whoever does not love abides in death. We know love by this, that he laid down his life for us—and we ought to lay down our lives for one another. How does God's love abide in anyone who has the world's goods and sees a brother or sister in need and yet refuses help? Little children, let us love, not in word or speech, but in truth and action.

1 JOHN 3:14, 16-18

Tuesday

His Mind in Us

Let each of you look not to your own interests, but to the interests of others. Let the same mind be in you that was in Christ Jesus, who, though he was in the form of God, did not regard equality with God as something to be exploited, but emptied himself, taking the form of a slave, being born in human likeness. And being found in human form,

he humbled himself and became obedient to the point of death—
even death on a cross.

PHILIPPIANS 2:4-8

Wednesday

In His Steps

Christ also suffered for you, leaving you an example, so that you
should follow in his steps. "He committed no sin, and no deceit
was found in his mouth." When he was abused, he did not return
abuse; when he suffered, he did not threaten; but he entrusted
himself to the one who judges justly. He himself bore our sins in
his body on the cross, so that, free from sins, we might live for
righteousness; by his wounds you have been healed. For you were
going astray like sheep, but now you have returned to the shepherd
and guardian of your souls.

1 PETER 2:21B-25

Maundy Thursday

The Lord's Supper

While they were eating, Jesus took a loaf of bread, and after blessing
it he broke it, gave it to the disciples, and said, "Take, eat; this is my
body." Then he took a cup, and after giving thanks he gave it to them,
saying, "Drink from it, all of you; for this is my blood of the covenant,
which is poured out for many for the forgiveness of sins. I tell you, I will
never again drink of this fruit of the vine until that day when I drink it
new with you in my Father's kingdom."

MATTHEW 26:26-29

Good Friday

The Three Hours

[No short reading suffices today, when of all days we should fast and confess our sins. Go to church. Hear the story and accept his sacrifice. If duty detains you, meditate on the Passion: Repeat and think upon: "I live by faith in the Son of God, Who loved me and gave himself for me."]

Holy Saturday

Resting in Hope

I keep the L<small>ORD</small> always before me; because he is at my right hand,
    I shall not be moved.
Therefore my heart is glad, and my soul rejoices;
    my body also rests secure.
For you do not give me up to Sheol, or let your faithful one
    see the Pit.
You show me the path of life. In your presence there is fullness of joy;
    in your right hand are pleasures forevermore.

P<small>SALM</small> 16:8-11

Prayers

For Courage

O Thou who art heroic love, keep alive in our hearts that adventurous spirit, which makes people scorn the way of safety so that thy will be done. Amen.

For Real Religion

O Lord Christ, whose kingdom is not in word but in power, grant that even as we desire thine appearing among us, we may labor and pay our part of the cost, by the help of thy Holy Spirit. Amen.

For Endurance

Teach us, good Lord, to serve thee as thou deservest; to give and not to count the cost; to fight and not to heed the wounds; to toil and not to seek for rest; to labor and not to ask for any reward, save that of knowing that we do thy will; through Jesus Christ our Lord. Amen.

For a New World Order

O Lord Jesus Christ who biddest thy Church to bring all to thyself and to make all humankind one family in thee, make clear to each one of us to do our part in the task. Fire our minds with a vision of a more perfect society here on earth in which justice and right, peace and servanthood shall reign according to thy will, and help us, each one, O Lord, to do our part in this Forward Movement, that thy will may be done on earth as it is in heaven. Amen.

Almighty God, whose Son Jesus Christ came to cast fire upon the earth, grant that by the prayers of thy faithful people, a fire of burning zeal may be kindled and pass from heart to heart, that the light of Thy Church may shine forth bright and clear; through the same Thy Son Jesus Christ our Lord. Amen.

For the Whole Church

0 Eternal God, who by thy Son Jesus Christ didst establish the family of thy Church in all the world; Breathe upon it anew the gifts of thy Holy Spirit, that, awakening to thy command, it may go forth in lowly service yet in conquering might to win mankind to the love of thy Name; through our only Saviour Jesus Christ. Amen.

About
Forward Movement

Forward Movement inspires disciples and empowers evangelists. We live out our call as a discipleship ministry by publishing daily reflections and online resources. People around the world read daily devotions through *Forward Day by Day*, which is also available in Spanish (*Adelante Día a Día*) and Braille, online, as a podcast, and as an app for your smartphone.

A ministry of the Episcopal Church since 1935, Forward Movement is a nonprofit organization funded by sales of resources and gifts from generous donors.

Learn more about Forward Movement and our work, at forwardmovement.org or venadelante.org.